T0062234

GOD'S PLAN

WHAT EVERY CHRISTIAN SHOULD KNOW

DAN MALCZEWSKI

WESTBOW
PRESS

WestBow Press books may be ordered through booksellers or by contacting:

WestBow Press
A Division of Thomas Nelson
1663 Liberty Drive
Bloomington, IN 47403
www.westbowpress.com
1-(866) 928-1240

ISBN: 978-1-4497-0340-0 (sc)
ISBN: 978-1-4497-0341-7 (hc)
ISBN: 978-1-4497-0339-4 (e)

Library of Congress Control Number: 2010931004

Printed in the United States of America

WestBow Press rev. date: 9/24/2010

I would like to dedicate this manuscript to the people who made this many-year endeavor worthwhile: my wife, Janet, my son, David, and my daughters Cheryl and Leigh Heinze. They have read through this entire document and provided me with many criticisms, suggestions, and recommendations. Even more so, they have put up with my many mood swings and the continual bothersome pestering that accompanied this work. I sincerely thank them.

Contents

Introduction

After high school, I went directly to work. This occurred in the tumultuous 1960s. I enrolled in evening college and soon became acutely aware that something was wrong in our country. There were riots on college campuses, bombings, and sex, drugs, and rock and roll were being glorified all in the name of ending the war in Vietnam. While supposedly being against a foreign war, students were causing a domestic war on our own soil. Even though I was a committed atheist and evolutionist, I soon realized that even my professors were lying to me. At work, I was introduced to a fellow worker who was in the John Birch Society. He convinced me, and my wife, that all of society's turmoil was caused by communist professors on the college campuses, and we both joined. Interestingly, almost all of the other members were born again Christians, and my wife and I soon became convinced that our lives were being wasted on the cares of this world.

After my wife and I were first saved on the same day over forty years ago, our feet didn't touch the ground from the joy of our finding the Lord for almost a full year. We listened attentively to Christian radio stations almost obsessively. When contradictions began to crop up, I became confused and bewildered. My feet once again reached the ground. I prayed and read my Bible for answers.

Even though my most pressing issues were answered this way, I still felt unsatisfied so I decided to go to Christian bookstores and buy lots of books. I soon learned that there were many false teachers of Christianity out there who wrote prolifically. Since these people claimed to be true Christians, Christian bookstores were constrained to sell their books alongside true Christian authors. After a lot of reading and a lot of money invested, I began to discover which authors I could trust. Their books led me to other authors. After awhile, I had a completely trustworthy list of authors to rely upon. As my knowledge increased, my questions began to get answered.

One of the more pressing questions that I felt I needed an answer for was that if I were a Jew living at the time of Jesus in the land of Israel, would I have recognized Jesus as the Son of God and as Israel's Messiah? Even though I'm an avid reader, I still haven't been able to completely convince myself that I would have.

> Who hath believed our report? and to whom is the arm of the LORD revealed? For he shall grow up before him as a tender plant, and as a root out of a dry ground: he hath no form nor comeliness; and when we shall see him, there is no beauty that we should desire him. (Isa 53:1,2)

This Old Testament passage is, clearly, a prophecy of Jesus. How, according to this passage, would I ever have been able to recognize Him? Even the leading Jewish scholars of His day rejected Him. But, as I've discovered over the years, there was a clear way to identify Him. Using this biblical tool, I'd like to pass it on to you. When once I was about 30 percent certain that I could recognize Him, I am now more than 95 percent sure!

Based on many years of reading and praying, I have now amassed some knowledge and experience of Christianity that I'd like to pass on to other Christians who have not yet had the time to absorb the many wonderful treasures that true Christianity (and its author, Jesus) possesses. This treatise, then, is an attempt to convince born-again (i.e., sure of resurrection) Christians that their beliefs are certain and provable. It is also an attempt (hopefully a successful one) to show them how to read and understand God's inestimably wonderful Word. By doing so, it will give them the confidence that their beliefs and hopes are assured. It will also strengthen their standing against the assaults of unbelief. As such, it will demonstrate that Christians should not give up their intellect once they've embraced Christianity. I also, in every sense, pray that I have given God (and especially Jesus) all of the honor, reverence, and glory that He so assuredly deserves.

As I have previously stated, I also wish to pass on some of the knowledge I've gained through my years of reading and experiences. In this way, a brand, new Christian might be able to bypass some of the many years I've invested in learning. Hopefully, it will bring new Christians up to date with this knowledge. This book, however, contains very little new material as attested to by the many authors, and their works, that I allude to here. Rather, it is merely a potpourri of facts and ideas that I've collected over time.

It is also an attempt to reach the unbeliever by convincing him that Christianity doesn't require one to give up his mental faculties simply because of faith. In fact, simple logic, the true scientific method, and factuality actually *confirm* the truths claimed by Christianity.

I have included in this document many of the names and authors of books that have helped me. I pray that you too will be blessed by these many references. Furthermore, many of these references have attempted to demonstrate that the foundations of Christianity have not only withstood the test of time but also have stood up against so-called scientific scrutiny. What many believers fail to understand is that disputations, "falsely so called", are not written in stone or are not really "scientific" when held up to the mirror of the scientific method.

As Christians, we are *commanded* to defend our faith!

> **Beloved, when I gave all diligence to write unto you of the common salvation, it was needful for me to write**

unto you, and exhort you that ye should earnestly contend for the faith which was once delivered unto the saints. (Jude 1:3)

This book, then, is hopefully one useful tool that can provide the impetus towards that goal.

Most of what I have written is merely an introduction to some very profound topics. Because I wish to outline the entire scope of Scripture, I must almost insist that a Christian who wishes to learn more either use the reference material or get hold of some good Bible commentaries. My wish here is that most of the salient points of the Bible are covered at least cursorily. I further believe that any true Christian must always ask the toughest questions imaginable and then seek the information required to answer them. We should never leave any stone unturned.

I have attempted to provide reference material directly into the text in order to keep the reader's attention affixed to the direct subject matter. Too often while reading interesting Christian material, I have been bombarded by a multitude of superscripts, footnotes, index material, etc. Once I had shifted my attention to look these up, I lost my perspective upon return to the main text and had to be retuned to what I was reading before. As such, I have tried to avoid this cruel "research paper" style.

I have also included a bibliography with (what I hope will be) helpful notes. Without reading much of the material included in the bibliography, the Christian will lose much of the force of these authors' arguments contained herein which I have only cursorily presented.

As a last item of importance, I must insist that all honest people read the entire Bible at least once. This should be because of the historic importance of God's Word; it has changed lives all over the globe throughout the centuries. Furthermore, no honest critique should ever be leveled against a book which one has never read. No one of us would ever go to a used-car lot and literally believe whatever the salesman told him. We would do some research and come to our own conclusions. Likewise, we owe it to ourselves to honestly read the Bible and not to accept what other critics have said. Should we decide against the Scriptures, then we are solely responsible for our own decision. If we accept the Bible as inspired by God, then we should look to its Author as someone Who deserves our worship. As Harold Willmington of Liberty University states in one of his courses, the greatest compliment someone can give to an author is to say, "Hey, I read your book." As Christians, we should read through the Bible multiple times because this is the means God uses to communicate to us. Since the Bible can be, at times, very difficult to read, I repeat that I hope this book will be a useful tool to open the pages of the Scriptures to understanding and knowledge.

All biblical quotations in this book are taken from the King James Version.

I sincerely believe that God's plan, as presented here, is quite probably His correct plan for mankind and all of His creation. Once I have presented it, I will go over how it affects all of human history and the future. But first, let's get some preliminaries out of the way.

Chapter 1

KNOWLEDGE

Because we must start somewhere, I've chosen to attempt to convince the Christian of the importance of knowledge to further our understanding of God's plan for each of us. Just because we may be "Christians", nowhere does the Bible require us to forego our mental faculties. God, in fact, created us with the ability to know and understand.

Knowledge is the ability to retain facts. Facts are things we realize through our five senses; they are things we know to be true. Those things that we can all see, touch, smell, taste, and feel can be labeled as facts. The sun comes up every day; bluebirds are birds that are blue; vegetables grow in soil. Of course, certain senses such as smell, taste, and feel can be disputed. These arguments, however, are more a matter of individual preferences than they are a disputation over facts. We *assume* that everyone who experiences the same object for sight, sound, smell, taste, and touch all experience the same thing. Just as different people who see a frilly red dress in a department store window can dispute whether they believe that the dress is beautiful, we all assume that all these people see the dress exactly the same – as a frilly red dress. Philosophical, theoretical, and hypothetical arguments are not facts; they are polemics (i.e., logical arguments). Arguments, whether logical or illogical, cannot qualify as facts because an antithetical (i.e., a directly opposite) argument can have exactly the same appeal.

Knowledge is one of many ways to convert souls to Christ. Knowledge, however, is fraught with dangers. For example, Jesus' sacrifice on the Cross is illogical to the lost world.

> For the preaching of the cross is to them that perish foolishness; but unto us which are saved it is the power of God. For it is written, I will destroy the wisdom of the wise, and will bring to nothing the understanding of the prudent. Where is the wise? where is the scribe? where is the disputer of this world? hath not God made foolish the wisdom of this world? For after that in the wisdom of God the world by wisdom knew not God, it pleased God by the foolishness of preaching to save them that believe. For the Jews require a sign, and the Greeks seek after wisdom: But we preach Christ crucified, unto the Jews a stumblingblock, and unto the Greeks foolishness; But unto them which are called, both Jews and Greeks, Christ the power of God, and the wisdom of God. Because the foolishness of God is wiser than men; and the weakness of God is stronger than men. For ye see your calling, brethren, how that not many wise men after the flesh, not many mighty, not many noble, are called: But God hath chosen the foolish things of the world to confound the wise; and God hath chosen the weak things of the world to confound the things which are mighty; And base things of the world, and things which are despised, hath God chosen, yea, and things which are not, to bring to nought things that are: That no flesh should glory in his presence. But of him are ye in Christ Jesus, who of God is made unto us wisdom, and righteousness, and sanctification, and redemption: That, according

as it is written, He that glorieth, let him glory in the Lord. (1 Cor 1:18-31)

So we can see that wisdom (i.e., knowledge) is not to be relied on for our Salvation.

Now as touching things offered unto idols, we know that we all have knowledge. Knowledge puffeth up, but charity edifieth. And if any man think that he knoweth any thing, he knoweth nothing yet as he ought to know. But if any man love God, the same is known of him. (1 Cor 8:1-3)

Knowledge, furthermore, provokes conceit. God hates conceit because conceit is part of human pride. Human pride, in turn, makes us believe that we're just as smart as God or smarter than others.

Is there, then, any role for knowledge in Salvation? There must be! If God has Created everything, surely there must be some way to "prove" His existence. And how can we "prove" His existence without knowledge? How can so many professional scientists become convinced of God's love without knowledge (Of all the professions, scientists are the most prolific at accepting a belief in the existence of God and then moving on to acceptance of Salvation in Christ. Which profession is the least likely to accept Salvation in Christ? Theologians!)? Furthermore, the Bible tells us that knowledge is invaluable for Christians.

Prove all things; hold fast that which is good. (1Thes 5:21)

My people are destroyed for lack of knowledge: because thou hast rejected knowledge, I will also reject thee, that thou shalt be no priest to me: seeing thou hast forgotten the law of thy God, I will also forget thy children. (Hosea 4:6)

My son, if thou wilt receive my words, and hide my commandments with thee; So that thou incline

> thine ear unto wisdom, and apply thine heart to understanding; Yea, if thou criest after knowledge, and liftest up thy voice for understanding; If thou seekest her as silver, and searchest for her as for hid treasures; Then shalt thou understand the fear of the LORD, and find the knowledge of God. For the LORD giveth wisdom: out of his mouth cometh knowledge and understanding. He layeth up sound wisdom for the righteous: he is a buckler to them that walk uprightly. He keepeth the paths of judgment, and preserveth the way of his saints. Then shalt thou understand righteousness, and judgment, and equity; yea, every good path. (Prov 2:1-9)

But knowledge and wisdom are to be handled carefully with all humility.

> Who is a wise man and endued with knowledge among you? let him shew out of a good conversation his works with meekness of wisdom. But if ye have bitter envying and strife in your hearts, glory not, and lie not against the truth. This wisdom descendeth not from above, but is earthly, sensual, devilish. For where envying and strife is, there is confusion and every evil work. But the wisdom that is from above is first pure, then peaceable, gentle, and easy to be intreated, full of mercy and good fruits, without partiality, and without hypocrisy. (James 3:13-17)

The knowledge of the existence of God and His Gospel must move the 18 inches from our heads to our hearts. There is a general kind of knowledge of many things, and there is biblical knowledge. Biblical knowledge is saving knowledge. General knowledge makes us conceited; biblical knowledge produces humility. Proper (i.e., biblical) knowledge validates truth. The unadulterated truth leads to Christ. Christ leads us to His Gospel.

> The fool hath said in his heart, There is no God. They are corrupt, they have done abominable works, there is none that doeth good. (Ps 14:1)

Notice that the fool says this in his heart – not his mind!

Knowledge not only can lead us to the truth (so long as we're honest with ourselves), but it can also defend the truth of the Scriptures. Christians who study such a defense are called "apologists" from the Greek word "apologia" which means an answer or a defense. Christian apologists take their authority for their defense of Scripture from basically two passages.

> But sanctify the Lord God in your hearts: and be ready always to give an answer to every man that asketh you a reason of the hope that is in you with meekness and fear: (1 Pet 3:15)

> Beloved, when I gave all diligence to write unto you of the common salvation, it was needful for me to write unto you, and exhort you that ye should earnestly contend for the faith which was once delivered unto the saints. (Jude 1:3)

We, as Christians, should always be ready to give an answer for our belief in Christianity to anyone who asks. We're also *required* to defend our Christianity against all of the attacks leveled by unbelief.

Unfortunately, too many Christians have no idea how to explain Christianity. This is because they have become comfortable in their beliefs. While there's nothing necessarily wrong with this, they miss out on some of the more wonderful truths of Christianity.

> And ye shall know the truth, and the truth shall make you free. (John 8:32)

Even though we've used the words "wisdom" and "knowledge" somewhat interchangeably, there is a marked difference in the meanings of the words. Knowledge is the ability to retain facts.

These facts could be trivial, unrelated facts. Wisdom, on the other hand, is the ability to use knowledge in a coherent, logical manner. Someone could be very knowledgeable and not wise. On the other hand, a wise person need not be knowledgeable. A wise person is always to be preferred over a knowledgeable one. Obviously, the best of both worlds would be to be both knowledgeable and wise.

From hereon, our use of the word "knowledge" shall be constrained to mean biblical knowledge. That is, the kind of knowledge that leads us to the truth. This is true wisdom. Biblical apologists use this kind of knowledge almost exclusively.

Too many Christians rely on "faith" alone. Many have never even read the whole Bible. But faith alone can be a "false" faith. Oftentimes when arguing with someone of a different belief, the argument always boils down to "faith". But faith in what? Muslims, Hindus, Mormons, etc. also claim to have "faith". Muslims will argue that they have faith in their prophet Mohammed, in their Koran, and in their god Allah. Hindus will argue similarly from their Vedas, and Mormons will argue from the Book of Mormon. But are Allah (the god of Islam), Brahmin (the Hindu god), and the Christ of Mormonism the same as the God of the Bible? Christians should know the answers to these questions. These answers involve knowledge.

Besides, God wishes us to *know* Him.

> Study to shew thyself approved unto God, a workman that needeth not to be ashamed, rightly dividing the word of truth. (2 Tim 2:15)
>
> For whoso findeth me findeth life, and shall obtain favour of the LORD. (Prov 8:35)
>
> O the depth of the riches both of the wisdom and knowledge of God! how unsearchable are his judgments, and his ways past finding out! For who hath known the mind of the Lord? or who hath been his counsellor? Or who hath first given to him, and

> it shall be recompensed unto him again? For of him, and through him, and to him, are all things: to whom be glory for ever. Amen. (Rom 11:33-36)

Knowledge of God's Word can keep us from sinning against Him.

> Thy word have I hid in mine heart, that I might not sin against thee. (Ps 119:11)

As we gain knowledge, we also reinforce our own faith. Too often, Christians simply accept things without question. If the Bible is God's Word, then it contains no contradictions. How, then, can the Christian resolve "an eye for an eye, a tooth for a tooth" from the Old Testament with Jesus' command to "turn the other cheek" from the New Testament? Is this truly a contradiction, or can it be resolved with the proper knowledge of biblical truths?

Once again, we need knowledge in order to convert the lost. Too often, unbelievers will question our beliefs with questions that most Christians can't answer.

Also, we need knowledge to become Christian apologists to defend our faith from the onset of attacks from the unfaithful.

This all comes down to one, searching problem. Christians, above the rest of humanity, should continually ask questions of their faith that some might think are embarrassing. For example, how could a God of love send a universal Flood to wipe out all of humanity except for Noah's immediate family? How could He also instruct the Jews to kill all the men, women, children, and animals of certain tribes when the Jews returned to Israel from Egypt? Surely the *children* were innocent. These questions haunted me for the longest time until God revealed to me the answers I needed. The answer to this will be addressed later.

One interesting aspect of Christian apologetics lends itself to the tremendous increase of knowledge that we find ourselves in today. It seems that, as we get closer to our Lord's return, God is revealing Himself to us in more and more ways. Anyone who is honest and objective enough to recognize this must realize that all of the material contained in this book cannot be mere happenstance. For example, I sincerely believe that God will allow the Ark of the Covenant, the Ark portrayed in the movie The Raiders of the Lost Ark, to be discovered. Any true, Christian apologist who can arm himself with just the material presented herein should be able to present, and defend, the truths of Christianity very ably.

Getting back to the question of my ability to recognize Jesus as Israel's Messiah and the Son of God, I began to ponder what Jesus did to allow me, or anyone else, to recognize Him. For one thing, Jesus performed many miracles. Was this the one thing that I could count on to recognize Him? Not at all!

New Agers claim that Jesus, during the silent years not described in the Bible, went to India to study from the gurus and to Tibet to study from the monks. From these sources New Agers believe that Jesus was taught how to perform miracles. Some New Agers, who have been converted to Christianity, claim that there was, indeed, such a man who traveled to these locales as Jesus. His name was Apollonius of Tyana, Turkey. These ex-New Agers claim that Apollonius was Satan's counterfeit Christ. He performed miracles just as Jesus had. In fact, his name is recorded in Scripture.

> **And they had a king over them, which is the angel of the bottomless pit, whose name in the Hebrew tongue is Abaddon, but in the Greek tongue hath his name Apollyon. (Rev 9:11)**

This passage describes the angel of the bottomless pit in the Book of Revelation. Notice that in the Hebrew his name is "Abaddon", and in the Greek his name is "Apollyon". Both of these words translate into the English as "Destroyer". Interestingly, this biblical name in Latin is Apollonius!

Furthermore, a Christian by the name of Tal Brooke, in his book Lord of the Air, has written about his '60s experiences in college and beyond. It seems that Mr. Brooke decided that he could experiment with the hallucinogen, LSD, at many times the normal dosage. He relates that this experience opened his eyes to the brightest, most beautiful colors imaginable. He also saw unicorns, satyrs, and other mythical beasts. He also claims that he saw, and experienced, "god". Because of this experience, he wished to know more. So he traveled to India to become a surrogate of Sai Baba, perhaps the most powerful guru who ever lived. Sai Baba could make things materialize out of thin air, make things disappear into thin air, cure the most incurable of diseases, etc. Mr. Brooke relates that he experienced all of these miracles while entirely sober and completely free of the influence of any drugs. Eventually, Sai Baba's behavior began to take a more sinister and evil tone that alerted Tal to his evil nature. When Mr. Brooke finally became saved, he realized that Sai Baba's powers were vested in him demonically.

So we see that Jesus wasn't the only one who could perform "miracles". Obviously, Satan, his fallen angels, and demons could also perform miracles.

If Jesus' miracles would not suffice to identify Him, what else could? Let's allow the Scriptures to tell us.

> Remember the former things of old: for I am God, and there is none else; I am God, and there is none like me, Declaring the end from the beginning, and from ancient times the things that are not yet done, saying, My counsel shall stand, and I will do all my pleasure: (Isa 46:9-10)

God knows the future! He also is willing to make known His knowledge to us. This is called *prophecy.*

> For we have not followed cunningly devised fables, when we made known unto you the power and coming of our Lord Jesus Christ, but were eyewitnesses of his majesty. For he received from God the Father honour and glory, when there came such a voice to him from the excellent glory, This is my beloved Son, in whom

> I am well pleased. And this voice which came from heaven we heard, when we were with him in the holy mount. We have also a more sure word of prophecy; whereunto ye do well that ye take heed, as unto a light that shineth in a dark place, until the day dawn, and the day star arise in your hearts: Knowing this first, that no prophecy of the scripture is of any private interpretation. For the prophecy came not in old time by the will of man: but holy men of God spake as they were moved by the Holy Ghost. **(2 Pet 1:16-21)**

This passage comes from the Apostle Peter. He mentions that he personally witnessed God, the Father, telling all the witnesses at Jesus' baptism in the Jordan River that Jesus is His beloved Son. He also witnessed the glory of Jesus at the Transfiguration. After witnessing such powerful events, Peter tells us that prophecy is more important!

A careful investigation of Old Testament prophecies concerning Jesus point to Him, and Him alone, as both Israel's Messiah and God! We shall discuss these in more detail a little later in this book.

For those who have not received Jesus as their personal Savior and Lord, apologetics sets itself up as an arbiter of God's Word. If it can be successfully demonstrated that facts, science, and pure logic attest to the veracity of the Bible, then the unbeliever must reject the Bible, and Jesus, at his own peril. Since some of the Word is beyond the scope of proof (e. g., the Creation), if those things that can not be shown to be true are at least probabilistically true (to a very high degree), then the reader should carefully, and objectively, consider them.

Now that we've covered the importance of logic, knowledge, and wisdom, it's time to set up some checkpoints for our further study.

Hermeneutics

Biblical hermeneutics are the ground rules for studying the Bible. In order to better understand the Bible, we must set some rules of incontrovertible interpretation. The very first rule we must set is how to understand the words written. Are they figurative, typological, symbolic, allegorical, or literal? If they're anything but literal, we at once place ourselves in the precarious position of relying on other, fallible men's interpretations. If more than one interpretation exists, then whose interpretation is to be relied upon? At least a literal interpretation can be tested on the basis of semantics, grammar, and context. All of these tests are terribly important. Context is the most elusive of these literal tests. Too often, people recite biblical verses out of context to justify their behavior. It's been said that a text taken out of context is a pretext.

There are other, pointed reasons why the literal text is to be preferred. For one, Jesus and the Apostles quoted from the Old Testament literally. For another, all fulfilled prophecy has been fulfilled literally. For another, God would not wish to offer His simple Plan of Salvation to mankind in a way that men could easily confuse. How then would God be able to judge us?

Another consideration must be given to the languages used in the Bible. The Bible was originally written in Hebrew, Aramaic, and Greek. These must assuredly be the languages in which the original text was inspired. This, however, presents a problem. There are hundreds of languages in the world. Unfortunately, there are many words in Hebrew, Aramaic, and Greek that cannot be easily translated into these other languages. Allow me to cite one simple example.

> **And to Seth, to him also there was born a son: and he called his name Enos: then began men to call upon the name of the LORD. (Gen 4:26)**

Seth was the believing replacement to Adam and Eve for the righteous Abel whom Cain murdered. Someone reading this passage would immediately believe that Enos, Seth's son, would continue in Seth's beliefs. If that's so, why would Moses (who wrote Genesis) include the second part of the sentence in this verse? It seems obvious that, because of Enos, men would call upon the name of the Lord. But why would men *begin* to call upon Him from Enos's line and not Adam's or Seth's? It is because this is a slight mistranslation. The Hebrew word translated "to call" is accurate. However, the Hebrew means "to call" in a *negative* sense. Chuck Missler translates the second part of the sentence of this verse as, "then began men to *profane* the name of the Lord." So we can see how a slight mistranslation can change our understanding of the Bible. Thus, Enos was responsible for introducing blasphemy to the ancient world.

These slight mistranslations should not deter us from attempting to read, and understand, the Bible. Does this mistranslation change the meaning and purpose of Salvation for anyone? I think not! Besides, true biblical scholars have pored over many of these slight mistranslations and concluded that none of them seem to occur when the Gospel is mentioned. Has God purposely preserved this part of the Bible for all to understand? You must be the judge of that.

While we're on the subject of translations, a brief word on biblical translations is in order. Because this study is undertaken in English, only English translations will be considered. There are several kinds of Bibles in view here: literal, contextual, and study. Literal Bibles are those that the translators have attempted to translate the ancient languages into English word-for-word. As already mentioned, this is not always an easy task because many of the original words may have multiple meanings in the English or no equivalent English meaning. The best known literal Bibles are the King James Version (KJV), New King James Version (NKJV), and the New American Standard Bible (NASB). The original King James Version was translated in 1611 and, as such, is written in the old English. While the translation has a beautifully poetic feel, it is sometimes very difficult to understand the text. Because it's been around so long, more concordances, topical bibles, commentaries, and dictionaries have been compiled for it than for any other

Bible. The New King James Version is merely the original King James Version with some new words substituted in the original. This was done for two reasons: readability and new discoveries of the definitions of some of the ancient words. The New American Standard Bible is a word-for-word translation in modern English. In fact, the NASB is a better literal translation than the KJV or NKJV. Contextual Bibles are attempts to recapture the original contexts and emotions surrounding the Word rather than the word-for-word translations. Most contextual Bibles do attempt to recapture all the original words used. Two of the best known contextual Bibles are the New International Version (NIV) and New Living Translation (NLT). The major problem with contextual translations is that we place ourselves at the mercy of the fallible (but probably sincere) men who translated them. Study Bibles are Bibles that contain a lot of explanatory marginalia, word studies, parenthetical explanations, maps, etc. Study Bibles are considered as such more on quantity rather than quality. Study Bibles also bridge the different translational Bibles such as the KJV, NASB, NIV, NLT, etc. Two of the better known study Bibles (of the hundreds) are the Scofield Bible and the Practical Application Bible. Once again, the student must place himself at the mercy of the translators' understanding of the text when reading the marginalia of a study Bible. A really good combination of the two (viz., a word-for-word study Bible) is probably the best compromise of all. I, myself, prefer the Liberty Annotated Study Bible (Thomas Nelson Publishers) which is a KJV study Bible. Even though the old English is sometimes very hard to understand, there are so many other references published for the KJV (because it's been around so long) that I can use whenever questions arise.

The next thing we must insist upon is that the Bible contains no contradictions in its original three languages. It cannot because God cannot lie.

> **God forbid: yea, let God be true, but every man a liar; as it is written, That thou mightest be justified in thy sayings, and mightest overcome when thou art judged. (Rom 3:4)**

If we think that we've encountered a contradiction, one, or more, of several possibilities present themselves. Firstly, we simply don't have enough information or knowledge to resolve the difficulty. Prayer and reading of the Scriptures are usually enough to clear up any problems for the truly curious. Secondly, a slight mistranslation could be confounding us. A good concordance, such as Strong's Concordance, could possibly ameliorate the problem. Thirdly, one, or more, of the problem passages may have been taken out of context. For example, the seeming contradiction between "an eye for an eye" and "turn the other cheek" resolves itself this way. The Old Testament injunction of "an eye for an eye, a tooth for a tooth" was a command to Israel's government to punish lawbreakers equally. It was never leveled to the individual. Jesus' command to "turn the other cheek" *was* a command to the individual. Thus, the government was instructed to punish lawbreakers without mercy, but the individual is to forgive those who wrong him.

One other resolution to difficult passages presents itself. There are very few passages in the Scriptures that stand alone. Very often parallel passages can explain themselves. For example, this curious passage appears in the Old Testament.

> Thou shalt not muzzle the ox when he treadeth out the corn. (Deut 25:4)

This is a command! It stands alone without explanation. What could it possibly mean? Thankfully, it is explained *twice* in the New Testament.

> For it is written in the law of Moses, Thou shalt not muzzle the mouth of the ox that treadeth out the corn. Doth God take care for oxen? Or saith he it altogether for our sakes? For our sakes, no doubt, this is written: that he that ploweth should plow in hope; and that he that thresheth in hope should be partaker of his hope. (1 Cor 9:9-10)

> Let the elders that rule well be counted worthy of double honour, especially they who labour in the word and doctrine. For the scripture saith, Thou shalt not muzzle the ox that treadeth out the corn. And, The labourer is worthy of his reward. (1 Tim 5:17-18)

A very interesting explanation, indeed!

The next thing we insist upon is that parables, allegories, types, etc. *never* introduce a new teaching. If the Bible was written for even the least intelligent of us, how could God expect us to understand such symbolism? The obvious answer is that He can't! But such symbols can expand upon an already expounded teaching. They are meant to illustrate parts of biblical teaching and are not to be taken too far. For example, the "prodigal son" parable of the New Testament (Luke 15:11-32) never mentions names. Are we to ask the participants' names? It is the story, without too much detail, that teaches us the importance of Salvation.

The final point I'd like to make when reading the Bible is to read and study it with the respect and authority it deserves as God's Word. We should humble ourselves when we apply its truths to our lives. We should also continue to remember all of God's many, infinite attributes when we study. Among these, but not limited to them, is omniscience (all-knowing), omnipotence (all-powerful), ubiquity (He is everywhere), all-loving, all-judgmental, etc.

These, then, are the minimal requirements we should adhere to when reading God's Holy Book. We summarize them below.

1. The Bible is its own authority and does not contradict itself.
2. The Bible is to be understood literally unless the context permits a figurative interpretation.
3. The Bible is to be understood in conjunction with God's attributes:
    a. He is omniscient
    b. He is immutable

   c. He is ubiquitous
   d. He is omnipotent
   e. He is ageless
   f. He is all-just
   g. He is all-loving

4. The Bible is inspired in its original three languages, but no translation is to be completely relied upon.
5. We compare Scripture with Scripture to understand God's revelations.

There are many other rules that can be imposed, but these should suffice for our study. For those wishing to learn more about biblical hermeneutics, I recommend that the reader search out and get a good book on this subject.

Chapter 2

CHRISTIANITY

In order to defend Christianity to others, we must first understand Christianity. There are many defenses for Christianity. Here we address just a few.

The Resurrection

Christianity claims to defend itself. One of the most important ways it does so is through the Resurrection of Jesus. Jesus predicted that He would die, be buried for three days, and be resurrected on the third day.

> Jesus answered and said unto them, Destroy this temple, and in three days I will raise it up. Then said the Jews, Forty and six years was this temple in building, and wilt thou rear it up in three days? But he spake of the temple of his body. When therefore he was risen from the dead, his disciples remembered that he had said this unto them; and they believed the scripture, and the word which Jesus had said. (John 2:19-22)

The Bible claims that many people witnessed Him after His Crucifixion.

> For I delivered unto you first of all that which I also received, how that Christ died for our sins according to the scriptures; And that he was buried, and that he rose again the third day according to the scriptures: And that he was seen of Cephas, then of the twelve: After that, he was seen of above five hundred brethren at once; of whom the greater part remain unto this present, but some are fallen asleep. (KJV, 1 Cor. 15:3-6)

As can be seen, Jesus was resurrected on the third day, and His appearance, after His death and resurrection, was witnessed by over 500 people. Furthermore, many contemporary historians report His resurrection.

An atheistic journalist, Frank Morison, desirous to disprove the claims of Christianity, decided to focus on the Resurrection. He became converted! He wrote a powerful, classic treatise on his conclusions called, Who Moved the Stone?. One of his most powerful conclusions he based on simple logic. There were only three parties who were interested in the possibility of Jesus' resurrection: the Jewish Sanhedrin (the ruling priestly body), the Romans, and Jesus' disciples. The first two parties were both committed to protecting Jesus' body so that the disciples could never claim that Jesus was resurrected. The disciples were in unbelief of Jesus' promises (except for John) which is easily attested to by the fact that they scattered to the four winds when Jesus was arrested. Once the tomb was emptied, the disciples had no interest in stealing Jesus' body. If Jesus had not been resurrected, the Jews and Romans simply had to produce His body. But, they couldn't! Furthermore, the disciples became so changed by the Resurrection that they were willing to face disgrace, mockery, and martyrdom. This is something they would never have done had they stolen the body. Many people are willing to die for a lie, but no one is willing to die for a lie that they know, for sure, is a lie. Therefore, the New Testament's account of the Resurrection must be true!

There are some people, and the Koran, that claim that Jesus didn't really die on the cross. Somehow, He was able to survive it. When this claim was given to a group of medical doctors, they immediately concluded that, according to the Bible's description of the Crucifixion such as blood and water pouring out of His side when He was pierced (viz., John 19:34), He was definitely dead.

The Resurrection is such a powerful argument for the veracity of Christianity that to simply disprove its validity is to disprove Christianity! No other religion in the world can make such a claim. If we simply take the claims of all the religions in the world as scientific theories, then each must stand the test of such theories. In Werner Gitt's excellent book, In the Beginning Was Information, he makes the following claim about scientific theories.

> It is not possible to verify a theory; a theory can only be falsified. A theory is good if it could be falsified very easily, and when it survives all open criticisms and tests, it can be accepted.

Since Christianity has survived every criticism and test, it must be accepted! No other religion can meet this criterion.

Jesus is God

Jesus' appearance on the scene in Israel was to offer Himself as their Messiah. This was predicted in the Book of Daniel.

> And whiles I was speaking, and praying, and confessing my sin and the sin of my people Israel, and presenting my supplication before the LORD my God for the holy mountain of my God; Yea, whiles I was speaking in prayer, even the man Gabriel, whom I had seen in the vision at the beginning, being caused to fly swiftly, touched me about the time of the evening oblation. And he informed me, and talked

> with me, and said, O Daniel, I am now come forth to give thee skill and understanding. At the beginning of thy supplications the commandment came forth, and I am come to shew thee; for thou art greatly beloved: therefore understand the matter, and consider the vision. Seventy weeks are determined upon thy people and upon thy holy city, to finish the transgression, and to make an end of sins, and to make reconciliation for iniquity, and to bring in everlasting righteousness, and to seal up the vision and prophecy, and to anoint the most Holy. Know therefore and understand, that from the going forth of the commandment to restore and to build Jerusalem unto the Messiah the Prince shall be seven weeks, and threescore and two weeks: the street shall be built again, and the wall, even in troublous times. And after threescore and two weeks shall Messiah be cut off, but not for himself: and the people of the prince that shall come shall destroy the city and the sanctuary; and the end thereof shall be with a flood, and unto the end of the war desolations are determined. (Dan 9:20-26)

Notice the use of the word "weeks". This word is actually the word for "sevens". The number "seven" is a holy number to the Jews. It can mean seven minutes, hours, days, weeks, years, etc. Daniel was reading the Book of Jeremiah just before this prophecy. In that book, Jeremiah clearly referred to sevens of years. Therefore, seventy "sevens" clearly means 490 years. Seven "sevens" and sixty-two "sevens" is just another way of saying sixty-nine "sevens" or 483 years. Why these 69 "sevens" are split between 7 and 62, I'm not sure. But this countdown to the coming of the Messiah (Messiah means "the Anointed One") commenced with the decree to restore and to rebuild Jerusalem. Archaeologically, this decree has been found! In Sir Robert Anderson's brilliant and classic work, The Coming Prince, he calculates the time from the time of the decree to Jesus' offering of Himself as Israel's Messiah.

> And when he was come near, he beheld the city, and wept over it, Saying, If thou hadst known, even thou, at least in this thy day, the things which belong unto thy peace! but now they are hid from thine eyes. (KJV, Luke 19:41-42)

According to Daniel, the Messiah would offer Himself to Israel 483 years from the decree. Sir Robert Anderson, in his classic work The Coming Prince, calculated this day as April 6, 32 AD. It was a specific *day* that all the Jews should have been aware of. This is a major reason that I believe I would've been able to recognize Jesus as the Messiah! We will calculate this day as Sir Robert Anderson does in the last chapter.

Jesus, by offering Himself as their Messiah, also claimed to be God! Other Scriptures authorize this rendering.

> For unto us a child is born, unto us a son is given: and the government shall be upon his shoulder: and his name shall be called Wonderful, Counsellor, The mighty God, The everlasting Father, The Prince of Peace. (Isa 9:6)

> Teaching us that, denying ungodliness and worldly lusts, we should live soberly, righteously, and godly, in this present world; Looking for that blessed hope, and the glorious appearing of the great God and our Saviour Jesus Christ; Who gave himself for us, that he might redeem us from all iniquity, and purify unto himself a peculiar people, zealous of good works. (Titus 2:12-14)

> When Israel was a child, then I loved him, and called my son out of Egypt. (Hosea 11:1)

The prophets and Apostles alike recognized Jesus as not merely the Messiah but also the Son of God.

It is the Resurrection, however, that puts God the Father's stamp of approval on Jesus' ministry. Sure, others have been resurrected in both the Old and New Testaments, but none of them had the power to resurrect *themselves*. Jesus did! If Jesus could resurrect Himself, then He has the power to resurrect *us*. This is called the "blessed hope" of Christianity. We have no such hope in any other religious figure. Mohammed, Brahmin, Buddha, Confucius, or any other person has ever been able to duplicate this feat.

> Moreover, brethren, I declare unto you the gospel which I preached unto you, which also ye have received, and wherein ye stand; By which also ye are saved, if ye keep in memory what I preached unto you, unless ye have believed in vain. For I delivered unto you first of all that which I also received, how that Christ died for our sins according to the scriptures; And that he was buried, and that he rose again the third day according to the scriptures: And that he was seen of Cephas, then of the twelve: After that, he was seen of above five hundred brethren at once; of whom the greater part remain unto this present, but some are fallen asleep. After that, he was seen of James; then of all the apostles. And last of all he was seen of me also, as of one born out of due time. For I am the least of the apostles, that am not meet to be called an apostle, because I persecuted the church of God. But by the grace of God I am what I am: and his grace which was bestowed upon me was not in vain; but I laboured more abundantly than they all: yet not I, but the grace of God which was with me. Therefore whether it were I or they, so we preach, and so ye believed. Now if Christ be preached that he rose from the dead, how say some among you that there is no resurrection of the dead? But if there be no resurrection of the dead, then is Christ not risen: And if Christ be not risen, then is our preaching vain, and your faith is also vain. Yea, and we are found false

> witnesses of God; because we have testified of God that he raised up Christ: whom he raised not up, if so be that the dead rise not. For if the dead rise not, then is not Christ raised: And if Christ be not raised, your faith is vain; ye are yet in your sins. Then they also which are fallen asleep in Christ are perished. If in this life only we have hope in Christ, we are of all men most miserable. But now is Christ risen from the dead, and become the firstfruits of them that slept. For since by man came death, by man came also the resurrection of the dead. For as in Adam all die, even so in Christ shall all be made alive. But every man in his own order: Christ the firstfruits; afterward they that are Christ's at his coming. Then cometh the end, when he shall have delivered up the kingdom to God, even the Father; when he shall have put down all rule and all authority and power. For he must reign, till he hath put all enemies under his feet. The last enemy that shall be destroyed is death. (1 Cor 15:1-26)

What a powerful argument! Only God has the power to resurrect Himself. Thus, once again, the power of the Resurrection is central to Christianity. These Scriptures should be read over and over again by every Christian until he is absolutely certain he understands them.

Higher Criticism, the Jesus Seminar, and the Media

Let's now discuss some of the main detractors of biblical truth. As we will see, all of their arguments against Christianity have been thoroughly and completely refuted. As a matter of fact, their negative arguments are so clearly erroneous, they actually confirm the truth of the Bible.

Over 100 years ago, a school of theology was opened in Germany to criticize the Bible. This school was called the School of Higher Criticism. At first, this school was highly acclaimed by theologians in the Protestant community because they deemed that by answering criticisms leveled by the school the arguments of Christianity would be strengthened. However, the school quickly devolved into pure criticism without excuse. Many of their claims became highly contrived arguments meant, obviously, just to discredit the Bible.

One of their claims was that the Old Testament was simply passed on by word of mouth until it was finally written down by Moses. They purposely predate other religious writings before the Pentateuch (Moses' five books). Because of this, they claim that Moses actually copied his stories from them. Could this claim possibly be true? Dr. Joseph Dillow, in his book The Waters Above, points out that these other religions that the Jews supposedly copied their religion from worshipped rocks, trees, streams, etc. They actually ascribed personalities and god-like qualities to them. Furthermore, all of their religions were polytheistic. Which makes more sense? Did the Jews copy their religion from them and then devolve into a monotheistic religion or vice-versa?

As for the claim that the Bible was passed down by word of mouth for generations before it was finally transcribed, we cite the following.

> **This is the book of the generations of Adam. In the day that God created man, in the likeness of God made he him; (Gen 5:1)**

Notice the word "book". Moses is actually saying that Adam had compiled an historic record of his offspring. The word "book" also appears in other places in Genesis. It is highly probable that Noah preserved Adam's (and other's) writings through the Flood and passed it down through generations that are no longer available today. What possible religion could possibly predate Adam's writings?

Another claim made by the "higher school" was that the Book of Isaiah was written by at least two authors because of "detectable" mood changes in the writing style in the book. This second, unidentified author they dubbed as deutero-Isaiah (or, second Isaiah) since they couldn't distinctly identify him. He supposedly added to Isaiah's original writing many years after Jesus' death and resurrection. Curiously, all of deutero-Isaiah's additions contain all of the prophecies regarding Jesus. In this way, the "higher school" eliminates all of Isaiah's *prophecies* making them history instead.

When the Dead Sea Scrolls were discovered in 1947, all of the books of the Old Testament, excluding the Book of Esther, were discovered at least in part. These books were dated about 200-300 B.C. In an almost divine refutation of the "higher school", the entire 66-chapter of the Book of Isaiah (called the Great Isaiah Scroll) was discovered. Remember, this entire book was obviously written at least 200 years before Jesus' birth. There couldn't have been a deutero-Isaiah! No disclaimer or apology has ever come forth from the "higher school". This falsehood is still in circulation and has been fairly successful at deceiving the uninitiated. But for the knowledgeable, the "higher school" has actually rendered them a favor: they've clearly identified all of Isaiah's messianic prophecies.

There are many other claims that the "higher school" has issued that have since been demonstrated to be false. To this day, no retraction has ever been forwarded by the school.

The Jesus Seminar is a group of loosely knit "theologians" who offer opinions on Jesus' life and ministry. I placed the word theologian in quotes because only some of these people have degrees and even fewer have any true, professional acquaintance with the Bible. These self-appointed "scholars" continually criticize the meanings of Jesus' ministry. They usually base their conclusions on the Gnostic Gospel of Thomas. This book claims to fill in many of the unknown gaps in Jesus' life and contains direct "quotations" from Jesus. The Gnostics were self-proclaimed "Christians" who declared that their Christianity is based on superior knowledge. Hence the name Gnostic which is Greek for "knowledge". They didn't believe in Jesus' deity or mission. But they did write many books some of which are known as pseudepigraphics (or "false writings"). These are books which are written and claimed to be written by another author. Almost all of these books were written at least 300 years after Jesus and the Apostles. This is the case for the Gospel of Thomas, which is claimed to be written by the Apostle Thomas ("doubting" Thomas). The Apostle Thomas was obviously dead when this writing was compiled. The Apostles, and those who studied under them, wrote many scathing comments on the Gnostics, whom they believed were heretics and were trying to undermine the Christian faith.

The Jesus Seminar has made many criticisms of Jesus' life that counters classical Christianity. Using the Gospel of Thomas, they have challenged many of Jesus' words written in the classical Gospels and have even forwarded their own Bible with their own analysis of what Jesus could have actually said in the Gospel of Mark. Curiously, only two of Jesus' quotations were probably actually said by Jesus in their estimation. When it comes down to Jesus, the major media outlets always seem to seek out these people. Specials are produced for TV such as "The Historical Jesus" based on the Jesus Seminar's input. Instead of seeking out true biblical scholars for their input, the media proves their atheistic bias against Christianity.

The media has long shown their hatred of Christianity in their TV, movies, and newspaper outlets. Some years ago, CBS put on a special movie on Noah's Flood. In the movie, there were pirates in the water! This depiction of the Flood would have been laughable had it not achieved its intended function of deceiving masses of people of the true, biblical account. Movies, such as "The Last Temptation of Christ", have depicted Jesus in various, unbiblical ways. Whether depicting Him as a coward, married man, or homosexual seems not to matter to the Hollywood crowd. Most of these movies were produced by former, disgruntled priests, outright atheists, homosexuals, etc. But the truth does not matter to Hollywood. The backgrounds of these producers are never publicized. This achieves the desired result of deceiving people who are unaware of the biblical accounts.

Probabilities

Probabilities offer another way to confirm the veracity of Christianity. Even though probabilities that offer a fairly even chance of success can be mere guesswork; probabilities that tend to zero or one are surer of a predicted outcome since they predict almost absolute failure or absolute certainty of an event. These should be seriously considered by the open-minded Christian.

Before we begin a discussion of probabilities, another concept must be introduced. This concept, taught in mathematics, concerns the idea of *limits*. Limits concern themselves with what value a formula approaches as the variable(s) in the formula approach a value. For example, the simple equation y = 2x approaches a limit for y (or 2x) as a limit for x is approached. As x approaches the value 3, y approaches the value 2x = 2*3 = 6. As x approaches the value 5, y approaches the value 2x = 2*5 = 10. The value of y is the value of the formula (namely 2x in our example), and the value of x is the value of the variable. The value of the variable, x, determines the value of the formula, y. It is important to understand in the theory of limits that these values are never exactly reached; they are *essentially* reached. So when x approaches the limit of 3, at x = 2.9999999999, y = 2*2.9999999999 = 5.9999999, which is essentially the value of 6.

There is one limit that concerns us here. It is the limit of y = 1/x as x approaches infinity. Remember, infinity is not really a number; it simply means that x approaches larger and larger numbers to the point of inconceivability by human beings. So let's see what this limit is. To simplify our calculations, we'll simply use whole numbers for x. When x = 1, 1/x = 1/1 = 1. When x =2, 1/x = ½ = .5. When x = 3, 1/x = 1/3 = .333.... Skipping to x = 10, 1/x = 1/10 = .1. When x = 100, 1/x = 1/100 = .01. When x = 1,000,000, 1/x = 1/1000000 = .000001. As we can see, as the value of x increases, the value of 1/x decreases. In fact, mathematicians have concluded that as x increases infinitely, the value of 1/x goes *essentially* to zero. This concept and specific limit will be used in what follows.

Many biblical scholars have identified at least 60 different prophecies that Jesus' life fulfilled from the Old Testament. Chuck Missler, in his book Cosmic Codes, claims that he's identified at least 300! Let's use the more conservative figure of 60. If each of these probabilities such that He'd be born of a virgin (Isaiah 7:14), that He'd be born in Bethlehem (Micah 5:2), that He would ride into Jerusalem on an ass (Zechariah 9:9), that He would be sold for 30 pieces of silver (Zechariah 11:12), etc., were assigned an *extremely* conservative probability of occurrence of 1/10, let's calculate the total probability that all of these prophecies could occur for one man. The figure 1/10 means that one out of every ten men fulfilled each individual prophecy. Also, the figure 1/10 includes the concept of *randomness*. Randomness simply means that no one purposely rigged the outcomes. Also, the figure of 1/10 is truly a conservative figure. Have, for example, one out of every ten men been born of a virgin? Have one out of every ten men been born in Bethlehem? As ridiculous as these probabilities are, I shall stick to these ridiculous figures to demonstrate how quickly they build up.

Each of these prophecies is a *mutually exclusive* event. This means that the fulfillment of any prophecy does not affect the fulfillment of any other prophecy. For example, someone born of a virgin need not be born in Bethlehem. To calculate the probability of the occurrence of all 60 mutually exclusive probabilities coming true for one person, we multiply the probabilities. An example will demonstrate this. Let's shuffle a deck of cards and, thereby, introduce some randomness for any card drawn. Now probability theory assigns a probability value of the fraction of (number of successful outcomes)÷(number of all outcomes). It can easily be seen that all probabilities have values between 0 and 1. The value 0 means that the probability of a successful outcome has no chance of occurrence. Drawing the eleven of diamonds from a deck of playing cards has no successful outcome since there is no eleven of diamonds in the deck. The value 1 means that the probability of a successful outcome is absolutely certain. Drawing *any* card from a deck of cards has a probability of 1 since any card satisfies our criterion. Now suppose we decide to draw an ace from a deck. There are 4 successful outcomes since there are 4 aces in the deck. Since there are 52 cards in the deck, there are 52 possible outcomes. Thus, the required probability to draw an ace from a deck of cards is 4/52 = 1/13. This time, however, let's calculate the probability to draw a spade from the deck. Since there are 13 spades in a deck, the probability to draw a spade is 13/52 = ¼. To calculate the probability of drawing the ace of spades, we can either calculate the probability directly as 1/52 or multiply our mutually exclusive probabilities to draw an ace *and* a spade as 1/4*1/13 = 1/52.

Therefore, the probability of all 60 prophecies being fulfilled is 1/10*1/10*1/10…

60 times. This gives a total probability of $1/10^{60}$. To calculate the number 10^{60}, we simply write the number 1 followed by 60 zeroes. This is the number

10000000000000000000000000000000000000000000000000
00000000000.

Can we even *name* this number much like we'd name a million, a billion, a trillion, etc.? Remember, this is the number that goes in the denominator of 1/x for x equal to this number. If we consider more realistic probabilities, such as one in ten billion for someone born of a virgin and one in a hundred thousand for someone born in Bethlehem, then we have the limit of 1/x as x goes to infinity. For practical people, this is essentially zero! As an interesting aside, scientists, at one time, began to calculate huge numbers for things such as the number of stars in the universe, the distances between stars, etc. To answer these huge numbers, mathematicians invented a number which they believed, at the time, would never be surpassed. The number they came up with is 10^{100} which they called a googol. It's easy to see that even the ridiculously conservative estimate of 1/100 for each of these prophecies results in the number $1/10^{120}$ which is less than 1/googol! Chuck Missler's book Cosmic Codes gives some interesting insights as to how small these probabilities actually are. With such an unrealistic probability of all 60 of these predictions being fulfilled in one man, we're logically *forced* to the conclusion that Jesus fulfilled all of these prophecies supernaturally!

Archaeology

Many claims have been made to discredit the truth of Christianity historically. For example, the country of Assyria was claimed to be imaginary. For years this claim went unchallenged until the city of Nineveh was discovered. The Hittite empire, likewise, was claimed as a falsehood until it, too, was discovered. Pontius Pilate's existence as governor of Judea was also questioned until his name was uncovered recently on a stone as Israel's governor. Many archaeologists have learned from their mistakes and have been converted to Christianity. In fact, about two-thirds of the settlements mentioned in Genesis Chapter 10 have been discovered. This is the biblical chapter that records where the grandsons of Noah settled after the Flood. Genesis Chapter 10 has become so reliable to archaeologists that it's been dubbed as "The Table of Nations". No historical name or site mentioned in the Bible has ever really been successfully discredited. There have been so many finds that they are beyond the scope of this study. Once again, the Bible is vindicated. To find more, Nelson's Bible Dictionary, the magazine Biblical Archaeological Review, and Randall Price's The Stones Cry Out are highly recommended.

Astronomy

The field of astronomy has so many proofs of biblical veracity it's hard to know where to start. Immanuel Velikovsky's Worlds in Collision is the book that finally started me to question my atheistic and evolutionary viewpoints. Dr. Velikovsky had many doctorates of which he used none to compile his findings and conclusions. Because of his seeming anti-evolutionary stance, this book was banned from all the U.S. college campuses. So much for college being the meeting-place for all ideas! He began under the assumption that all myths and legends contain a germ of truth. If he could successfully compare myths and legends from all over the world, he may find similarities that could reveal the truth behind them. He also had to construct a timeline in order to determine when different myths and legends began. He felt he did this successfully enough to come to an astounding conclusion. This conclusion drove him to the realization that all the current cosmological theories (i.e., the nebular hypothesis of the creation of the universe and evolution of the creation of life) were wrong. He noticed that at one point in his timeline something was missing in all the writings beforehand but mentioned by all afterward. This is the planet Venus! All of the cultures of the world describe, in mythological terms, the struggle between Earth and Venus. The descriptions that Velikovsky found led him to believe that Venus was, at one time, a comet with a head approximately the same size as the Earth. Several times in the distant past these two bodies came to near-collision paths and affected many things in our history. One time, however, the two were on a head-on collision path. Because both were surrounded by powerful magnetic fields, the collision was averted when the two magnets eventually repelled each much like smaller magnets do when similar poles are placed close together. According to Roche's Limit, two equally-sized bodies on a collision path will repel each other at about 2.5 times the radius of the Earth, or about 10,000 miles out. This repulsion caused Venus' orbit, as a comet, to dissipate and become eventually caught by the Sun's gravity and settled into a planetary orbit. But the havoc of this collision on the Earth was monumental. The electric discharge between Earth and Venus caused the pillar of fire to temporarily impede the approach of pharaoh's army from killing the Jews. Because the poles were the same (positive or negative) all along a line of the Earth, waters repelled including the Red Sea. This accounts for the parting of the waters. The resulting burn of the carbohydrates of the comet's tail in the upper atmosphere easily accounts for manna. He even went so far as to predict certain things that would have to be true if his thesis were correct. All of them later proved to be true. Velikovsky covers these things and much more than I could easily relate. The reader owes himself, as a matter of sincerity and honesty, to read this classic work. The main point, however, is well taken: that these stories in the Old Testament probably happened exactly as recorded therein!

Think of it! If many of the Old Testament "miracles" actually happened as recorded, God, in His Creative and Omniscient attributes, must've set the universe in motion beforehand just so these events could occur. Thus, He would have set the comet Venus in motion just so that it would have a near-collision with earth at the right time. He would've had to know what the ramifications of a near-collision with earth would cause, and, just as importantly, He would've had to calculate the exact *timing* of such a catastrophe. Furthermore, He would also have had to know about Moses and the Jews *millennia* before it happened. And what about Moses? If Moses were an unbelievably gifted scientist, he would have had to know what effects a collision path of Venus with Earth would cause. Furthermore, his timing would have to be perfect; he would've had to know just when to raise his hand when the waters parted. He would also have to know where water and food was in the desert to sustain approximately 2 million Jews for 40 years! Unless he was the greatest genius who ever lived, the only plausible conclusion that reason suggests is that he was in direct communication with the only being in the universe who knows everything: God! Just because these events happened naturally doesn't mean that God wasn't behind them, directing and insuring the outcomes supernaturally.

In Grant Jeffrey's work, Creation, many points are forwarded to convince any truly honest reader of the truth of Creation. Scientists, impressed by the delicate balance required to sustain life, have coined the term the "anthropic principle". This means that every possible requirement to sustain life on the Earth has been met and has probably not been met anywhere else in the universe. For example, the Earth's distance from the sun, 93,000,000 miles, is crucial. Any closer and it would be too hot for life. Any farther and it would be too cold for life. The Earth's atmosphere is also unique from any other place observed in the universe and is perfectly suited for life. The fact that liquid water has never been observed in any quantity on any other planet, or moon, is also important for the existence of life.

Probably one of the most remarkable aspects of the "anthropic principle" is that, of all the other planets in our solar system,

Earth's orbit is almost perfectly circular. This is attested to by the fact that our solar year is almost exactly 365.25 days. All the other planets' orbits are elliptical. It's almost as if the original solar system consisted of only the Earth and the sun. This is in line with the biblical concept that the earth was made for man and man for the earth. Consider this following scenario. These other planets floated out in space. Once their paths came within the sun's gravitational pull, their original trajectories resisted the sun's pull and the planet sped past the sun. Their velocities eventually slowed until they were overcome by the sun's gravity and were pulled back. Then they would accelerate in the opposite direction until they were pulled back again and the whole scenario would repeat itself. This would cause elliptical (i.e., egg-shaped) orbits. Thus, the current, scientific theories about the creation of the solar system are without merit. Any study of the physics concept of angular momentum would require that all the planets would have the same kind of angular momentum (they would have the same velocity of spin depending on their radius, and their spin would be in the same direction) as the originator of their angular momentum (i.e., the sun). But the planets do not behave so well. Some rotate in opposite directions. One planet's axis of rotation is actually in the plane (or parallel) to its revolution about the sun!

Biology

Gregor Mendel has been accredited by the world of science as the "father of genetics". He made extensive research into crossbreeding different kinds of peas based on flavor, size, nutrition, etc. He eventually discovered that his crossbreeding experiments could only go so far and then the crossbred peas would revert back to the original parents.

Since Mendel made his discoveries, many other scientists have attempted to crossbreed life from every sphere imaginable: fruit flies, dogs, cats, wheat, horses, etc. They all had the same experiences: after much diversity, the things crossbred would either eventually revert back to the original parents or the new crossbreeds would be sterile (i.e., they couldn't reproduce).

What are kinds? Taxonomists have attempted to categorize certain "kinds" based on similarities. These "kinds" they called "species". One kind of animal or plant could not reproduce with another kind of animal or plant from a different species. For example, a poodle could reproduce with a great dane and produce a dog that had characteristics of both. Hence, poodles and great danes were of the same species. A dog and a cat, however, could never reproduce.

The Bible mentions "kinds" but never defines them.

> **And God created great whales, and every living creature that moveth, which the waters brought forth abundantly, after their kind, and every winged fowl after his kind: and God saw that it was good. (Gen 1:21)**
>
> **And God said, Let the earth bring forth the living creature after his kind, cattle, and creeping thing, and beast of the earth after his kind: and it was so. And God made the beast of the earth after his kind, and cattle after their kind, and every thing that creepeth upon the earth after his kind: and God saw that it was good. (Gen 1:24-25)**

Evolution teaches that "kinds", or "species", can eventually become other "kinds" or "species" through random events. This is called "speciation". We have just shown that nature allows no such random changes to take place even though minor changes have been observed within species. These minor changes, however, do *not* result in the birth of whole new species. God, in His infinite wisdom, would never allow speciation to occur.

This is not to say that biochemists are not "monkeying" around with DNA. In fact, they have been successful in cloning many different kinds of animals. They've probably also been successful in creating "chimeras". Chimeras are beasts that have characteristics of two or more separate animal species such as a lion with a hawk's head! It must be remembered, however, that these experiments are artificial; they have nothing to do with natural processes.

DNA is composed of four chemicals: A – adenine, C – cytosine, G – guanine, and T – thymine. What is so remarkable about this is that the four letters make up *all* the possibly diverse characteristics of any life form. Even more remarkable is that A is complementary to T and C to G. That is, A and T and C and G always appear together; there can never be A to C, A to G, T to C, or T to G. This makes every combination only one of two pairs! This is, essentially, binary code! But the entire strand is so complex and long that no one has ever successfully identified every possibility. The amount of information is so immense that a single strand of human DNA, if typed on paper using standard letter sizes, would stretch from the North Pole to the equator. Could anyone in his right mind believe that such complexity could be the product of random chance? Mutations to the DNA structure, furthermore, never introduce new information; they destroy existing information. As someone has rightly pointed out: it would be akin to a tornado sweeping through a junkyard and leaving a Boeing 747 jet in its wake!

Information Theory

Dr. Werner Gitt's excellent book In the Beginning Was Information, treats the latest scientific findings on "information". Information, as he defines it, is communicative. That is, it requires both an author and a recipient. In the book, he demonstrates that human communication is based on languages. Most languages have both a written and spoken form (some "primitive" languages have no written form). Of all the life forms on planet Earth, man is the only life form that seems to be capable of both.

> The evolutionary idea of an upward development of grunts and snorts to cultural languages through the primitive languages of aboriginal languages has been thoroughly refuted by comparative linguistics.

This, and a series of definitions and theorems that are carefully constructed throughout the book, eventually lead to the following conclusion.

> Johann Peter Sübmilch established in 1756 that man could not have invented language without having the necessary intelligence, and also that intelligent thought in its turn depends on the previous existence of speech. The only solution to this paradox is that God must have given human beings language as a gift.

Thus, the evolutionary proposal that languages began with a series of grunts and groans and have "evolved" into today's languages has been thoroughly refuted by information theory. So we see that information theory, if any sense is to be made of it all, leads us, once again, to a Creator: God.

Bible Codes

Bible Codes are a new, and controversial, way that many believe confirm the veracity of the Bible. Bible Codes are hidden messages embedded within the words of Scripture. These codes are found by means of Equidistant Letter Sequences (or ELSs). These ELSs are found by skipping a constant number of letters in the Bible until a meaningful message is uncovered. ELSs can be discovered by skipping letters either forward or backwards through the original Hebrew. Spaces are not counted.

If such codes are real, they cannot, logically, contradict the plain message presented in Scripture. So why should the Christian be concerned with them? I'll allow Chuck Missler's answer in his Cosmic Codes answer this.

> There are some serious concerns over the ELS codes. Among these, however, are some concerns which we feel are disturbingly myopic. There are some critics of the ELS codes who feel that God has nothing in His Word that the common person cannot understand. This places a strange constraint upon God. Some feel that the emergence of the codes places His truth into the restrictive hands of an elite who have the fastest computers and the latest software.

> But it is very myopic and naïve to infer that *only* things which can be understood by the rank and file are in God's Word. I would expect that His Word is unfathomable by our puny intellects, however enlightened. "While safe enough for a child to wade in, it is a reservoir deep enough for even an elephant to bathe in." If, indeed, it is the Word of God, would you expect it to be any less?
>
> Let us remember that while God is extremely jealous of His Name, there is one thing that He elevates *even above His Name:* His Word. Furthermore, there are many mysteries deliberately put there as challenges to man.
>
> **"It is the glory of God to conceal a thing: but the honour of kings is to search out a matter." (KJV, Proverbs 25:2)**

The modern idea of Bible Codes was begun by Michael Ber Weissmandl, a Slovakian Jew who lived during the Holocaust. His work was cut short when he was arrested for being a Jew. His work was revived when a team of three Israeli scientists, Doron Witztum, Eliyahu Rips, and Yoav Rosenberg, published a paper in the journal Statistical Science. Their paper identified the names of 34 notable Jewish sages of history along with either the dates of their births or deaths all from the Book of Genesis. Their work also included a statistical analysis of their findings. After these results were published, they were challenged to find the names and dates of either the births or deaths of another 32 rabbis. To their astonishment, all 32 were found for an incredible 66 in all!

The Bible Codes were popularized by Michael Drosnin in his book The Bible Code. Mr. Drosnin, a journalist, became a guest on many TV talk shows and claimed that he discovered a code that foretold of Yitzhak Rabin's assassination. This code revealed when, where, and by whom Rabin would be assassinated. He further claimed to warn the Prime Minister unsuccessfully. He made many other claims that are difficult to substantiate.

Grant Jeffrey and Yacov Rambsel, a converted Jew, also made ELS searches of Scripture. Rambsel searched for confirmation of Jesus' divinity. In his book Yeshua, he found many ELSs confirming his theory. What the Christian must know about this is that the Greek name, Jesus, is Yeshua in Hebrew and means "salvation". Astoundingly, Mr. Yambsel did all of this *manually*; no computer software was used for his search. He found Jesus' name encoded especially around Isaiah 53, the chapter in Isaiah that specifically prophesies of Jesus' life during His First Advent. Grant Jeffrey's book The Signature of God, made other claims about newly discovered ELS codes.

All of this attention to Bible Codes caused a furor amongst mathematicians and statisticians. Many claimed that ELS searches could be conducted on any large work of literature and discover similar messages. Works such as War and Peace should be searched for ELSs. Besides, they claimed, the statistics and probability established for the Bible Codes are wrong.

Jeffrey Satinover became intrigued over this whole furor. In order to satisfy his own curiosity, he enlisted the aid of Harold Gans, one of the world's top code breakers at NSA (National Security Agency). Mr. Gans created a test on his home computer to determine the reliability of the existence of the Bible Codes by referring to the original work conducted by Witztum, Rips, and Rosenberg. His computer finally reported a probability of 1 in 62,500 that the Bible Codes could have been random thus confirming their work. This whole story is related in Satinover's book, Cracking the Bible Code.

Finally, R. Edwin Sherman became engrossed in this whole scenario. He has done extensive research on the Bible Codes and compared them to ELSs found in War and Peace. His findings are astounding! He has published his findings and his statistical works in his book Bible Code Bombshell. Chapter 53 of the Book of Isaiah predicts the First Advent of Jesus. To date, there have been 1,600 2 to 40 letter ELSs centered on this chapter! *None* of these codes refute anything found in the Bible literally. Some of these codes, a very small minority, are impossible to understand based on our present knowledge of the Bible. As an example, one of the codes reads "Smile, I see Matthew there. Let go!" Another one reads "Kidron calmed down and went." Some of the codes that are in accord with literal Scripture actually shed more light on already known doctrines. For example, one ELS reads "Know who the chosen people are or God will be angry." What's ultimately revealing is that codes centered on Isaiah 53 name all the apostles except Judas, and mention Mary, Martha, Jesus, Lazarus, Annas, Pilate, etc by name.

Another interesting cluster was found around Ezekiel Chapter 37. This chapter is believed by many Orthodox Jews as predicting the rebirth of Israel. To this date, 295 codes have been found. Saddam Hussein, Osama bin Laden, and other Muslim terrorists are named outright in these codes. Other historical facts that are not listed in the forward, literal rendering of the Bible are also found herein.

Mr. Sherman has performed a seminal work that will be hard to refute either mathematically or theologically. Jews, subjected to codes that clearly declare Jesus as God and Messiah, must reject these messages at their own peril.

There are many rules that have been discovered when searching for ELSs. Sherman goes over many of these. For example, predictions of the future require a prior knowledge of what to search for. It seems apparent to me that the antichrist's name must definitely be encoded. But what do you search for? You almost must know his name beforehand to search for it. Once the antichrist appears on the scene, ELSs might very well confirm his identity.

To date, I know of no one who has attempted to apply these ELSs to the Greek New Testament. It would be interesting to discover what could be found in the Greek.

The New Age and the Occult

The New Age is an amalgam of all kinds of different religious beliefs including idol worship, pantheism, polytheism, and the occult (i.e., worship of demonic forces and Satanism). A definite link has been shown to exist between those who believe in UFOs and the occult (see Alien Intrusion by Gary Bates). There are all kinds of seemingly disparate New Age beliefs ranging from the ancient Celts, to Druids, to Earth worship, to shamanism, to witchcraft, to Satanism. However divergent their beliefs, they all commonly hate Christianity. As such, many compromises between these belief systems have occurred, and they have aggregately been working on common databases to undermine Christianity, its morals, and its beliefs. Constance Cumbey, in her book The Hidden Dangers of the Rainbow, points out many of these common characteristics and the compromises adhered to undermine Christianity. In fact, she says in her Preface:

> This book sets forth a small portion of my research findings. What will be difficult to fully convey is the sense of mounting horror I found while piercing this multitude of data together. It appears to culminate in a scheme both fulfilling the prophetic requirements for the antichrist as set forth in the Bible, and also matching Nazism down to use of swastikas.

If there truly is a Satan (which I earnestly believe), then he is familiar with the Christian Bible. He is keenly aware that Christianity teaches the concept of the Rapture. This is a "catching away" of all the *true* Christians from the Earth without ever experiencing death. More will be said about this later. Satan also realizes that he will be allowed to rule the Earth for a brief time. Even though all of Satan's followers will be left behind after the Rapture, many of the people that are left behind will not be either followers of Jesus or him. He, therefore, is left with the task of explaining away this disappearance of Christ's faithful to the multitudes left behind.

The major way that the New Age attacks this problem is evolutionary. They claim that the zodiacal Age of Pisces has reached its end, and the Age of Aquarius is just beginning. The Age of Pisces, they claim, was the age of superstitious religious beliefs. The new Age of Aquarius will bring in a new age of peace, harmony, and brotherhood. The old superstitions (i.e., religion) will be swept away. The only people who can partake of this new Age of Aquarius, however, are the "initiated". These initiates are the people who will evolve to a higher stage of evolution (called "homo noeticus") during Aquarius. They have even given themselves over to a New Age leader. They believe that the spirit of the New Age (which is within all of us) is called the "Christ consciousness". Jesus had this spirit, but so did Buddha and Mohammed. Their New Age leader will be called "the Christ" since he will have this "Christ consciousness" more than anyone who has ever preceded him. He will unite the world in a new age of economics, politics, and religion (the New Age religion, of course). Anyone who opposes him will be executed.

The religious, especially the Christian fundamentalists, are too stubborn and adamant in their beliefs to participate in this higher evolutionary process. Our space brothers will help in the world's conversion to the Age of Aquarius by surrounding the planet by thousands of undetectable space ships. In order to allow these stubborn fundamentalists to participate in this new age of harmony, the space ships will "beam up" (much like Star Trek) millions of these Christians to "reeducate" them. Thus, they will be gone from the planet all during the Age of Aquarius. Others who succumb to religious teachings and are left behind must be "cleansed". This is merely a polite way of saying they will be executed.

In The Hidden Dangers of the Rainbow, Constance Cumbey relates the following.

> The Movement has threatened violence and even extermination of Jews, Christians, and Moslems failing to cooperate with "Maitreya" and the New World Religion. The threat is contained in several places in the Alice Bailey writings and reiterated in the David Spangler writings, which state that those of us who refuse to accept the "Christ" will be sent to another dimension other than physical incarnation, out of physical embodiment, to another level of vibration where we will be happier!

Maitreya was an Indian; a Hindu guru living in England. Benjamin Crème, a leading spokesman for the New Age movement, attempted to pass Maitreya off to the world as the long-awaited Christ. Alice Bailey was the founder of a publishing company that was originally called "Lucifer Trust". When that name was not received as universally as had been hoped, she changed the name to "Lucis Trust", thus successfully camouflaging her original intentions. David Spangler was another New Age spokesman. Please note that the New Age wishes to wipe out the only three monotheistic religions: Judaism, Christianity, and Islam. Obviously, Hinduism, Buddhism, Taoism, Shintoism, etc. are immune from the wrath of the New Agers.

Interestingly, this is almost the precise teaching of the Bible. By attempting to undermine the biblical teaching, and meaning, of the Rapture, Satan's followers actually affirm it. Since no other religion teaches anything akin to the Christian doctrine of the Rapture, the New Age therefore *confirms* the truth of Christianity!

Constance Cumbey's The Hidden Dangers of the Rainbow should be read by every Christian. The parallels between the satanically inspired worship system and modern, Christian prophecy are simply too great to be ignored. In The Hidden Dangers of the Rainbow, Constance Cumbey outlines the similarities between Christian prophecy and New Age beliefs on pp. 77-83, the parallels between Nazism and New Age tenets on pp. 115-120, and an outline synopsis of the New Age in Appendix G. Even though some aspects of the New Age movement are somewhat outdated in The Hidden Dangers of the Rainbow, it is still a must-read since much of her revelations are still held by the New Age Movement. As much as I would've liked to include much of it in this book, it is still too massive to include in such an introductory overview as this one.

Gary Bates' book, Alien Intrusion, is an excellent guide to the claims of those who believe in UFOs. He objectively relates all the evidence that has been presented up to the present. At the end of the book, he makes an astounding discovery. UFOs have a very strong link to the occult. This is another must-read book for the serious Christian.

Let's tackle the ideas of UFOs, "ghosts", ESP, and all other spiritual phenomena once for all.

> **By the which will we are sanctified through the offering of the body of Jesus Christ once for all. (Heb 10:10)**

If Jesus died "once for all" then He died for *all* of God's rebellious creatures. Since He died on earth and only once, He didn't die on any other planet. Thus, there are no rebellious creatures on any other planet. There are, therefore, no aliens living "out there". The only other rebellious creatures are fallen angels.

> **For we know that the whole creation groaneth and travaileth in pain together until now. (Rom 8:22)**

The fallen angels (more on them later) and mankind make up the whole of God's rebellious creation. Thus, Jesus also died for them. But the fallen angels will not accept Jesus' free offer of salvation. With no aliens to account for UFO phenomena and the strong credibility of the reality of these encounters, the only creatures that could be responsible for UFOs are fallen angels. Thus, all UFO phenomena are demonic (i.e., fallen angels)! Those people who have honestly researched these encounters have been amazed at the strong occultic influence prevalent in UFO encounters. See Gary Bates' book Alien Encounters for proof of this. Demonic influence is also behind such topics as hauntings, ESP, Hindu miracles, and other spiritual phenomena.

Chapter 3

GOD'S PLAN

With some of the apologetics out of the way, it's time to edify Christians about their faith, and the wisdom of God's Word. The very first thing we must tackle is whether God actually has a Plan to redeem mankind to Him. For Christians, this is a no-brainer; God doesn't do anything without a Plan. To prove it, we must use God's Word, the Bible, to demonstrate it.

> **Remember the former things of old: for I am God, and there is none else; I am God, and there is none like me, Declaring the end from the beginning, and from ancient times the things that are not yet done, saying, My counsel shall stand, and I will do all my pleasure: Calling a ravenous bird from the east, the man that executeth my counsel from a far country: yea, I have spoken it, I will also bring it to pass; I have purposed it, I will also do it. (Isa 46:9-11)**

As God clearly says, He will do all that He has planned ("purposed"). Thus, He clearly tells us He has a plan. Furthermore, God loves mankind and will redeem us even though we're as insects in His sight.

> **When I consider thy heavens, the work of thy fingers, the moon and the stars, which thou hast ordained; What is man, that thou art mindful of him? and the son of man, that thou visitest him? (Ps 8:3-4)**

If God, therefore, has a Plan for mankind, what is it?

After years of studying the Scriptures, I believe that God has revealed His Plan to me. My understanding of God's Plan is more of a model. It is fraught with the possibility of human error. Just as the structures of the atom and the double helix of DNA are scientific models, I propose, here, what I believe God's Plan is. Remember, a model is meant to be explanatory of characteristics which are observable. It need not even be true! So long as the model continues to explain observation, it should be adhered to. If it fails to do so even once, the model must be either modified (if it can simply be done) or rejected. The model I propose is probably about 95% scriptural. The other 5% is definitely conjectured. Here goes!

The Bible tells us that God Created all things.

> **In the beginning God created the heaven and the earth. (Gen 1:1)**

This is a verse every Christian knows. But, we ask, in the beginning of what? True biblical scholars believe that this beginning refers to time. With this, I agree. God began His countdown from the beginning of His Plan to the end. There is possibly a gap of time between His Creation of the universe (the heavens) and His Creation of man.

The Angels

When He Created the universe, He also Created the angels. Why He created the angels cannot be known, but all of the angels were Created with specific tasks assigned to them. One of them was Created with more power, beauty, and wisdom than the others.

GOD'S PLAN

> Moreover the word of the LORD came unto me, saying, Son of man, take up a lamentation upon the king of Tyrus, and say unto him, Thus saith the Lord GOD; Thou sealest up the sum, full of wisdom, and perfect in beauty. Thou hast been in Eden the garden of God; every precious stone was thy covering, the sardius, topaz, and the diamond, the beryl, the onyx, and the jasper, the sapphire, the emerald, and the carbuncle, and gold: the workmanship of thy tabrets and of thy pipes was prepared in thee in the day that thou wast created. Thou art the anointed cherub that covereth; and I have set thee so: thou wast upon the holy mountain of God; thou hast walked up and down in the midst of the stones of fire. Thou wast perfect in thy ways from the day that thou wast created, till iniquity was found in thee. By the multitude of thy merchandise they have filled the midst of thee with violence, and thou hast sinned: therefore I will cast thee as profane out of the mountain of God: and I will destroy thee, O covering cherub, from the midst of the stones of fire. Thine heart was lifted up because of thy beauty, thou hast corrupted thy wisdom by reason of thy brightness: I will cast thee to the ground, I will lay thee before kings, that they may behold thee. (Ezek 28:11-17)

This "guardian cherub", who was obviously the power behind the king of Tyre, was Created with great power and wisdom until he was expelled from the "mount of God". This passage is obviously addressed to the being that is responsible for the king of Tyre's power because the king of Tyre was never in the Garden of Eden. More is said of him in Isaiah.

> How art thou fallen from heaven, O Lucifer, son of the morning! how art thou cut down to the ground, which didst weaken the nations! For thou hast said in thine heart, I will ascend into heaven, I will exalt my

> throne above the stars of God: I will sit also upon the mount of the congregation, in the sides of the north: I will ascend above the heights of the clouds; I will be like the most High. Yet thou shalt be brought down to hell, to the sides of the pit. (KJV, Isa 14:12-15)

The King James Version of the Bible calls this angel Lucifer which means "morning star". Other translations use this meaning of Lucifer. Whether this is his name or not, we cannot say for sure because all of the ancient names in the Bible have meanings. We will use this "name" as this angel's "name" from hereon because, as already mentioned, the New Age Movement uses this name for Satan. I should think that if anyone would know his name, it would be they.

Why was this angel imbued with such power, wisdom, and beauty? It seems that his identity as a "guardian cherub" might be a clue. Perhaps God assigned him the task of screening the multiple questions that the other angels had for God. If this is true, then all the other angels knew him.

Because he was puffed up by pride, he decided that he was smart and powerful enough to occupy God's Throne, which he coveted. So he decided to overthrow God by secretly convincing his angels to rebel against Him. In fact, he succeeded in convincing 1/3 of the angels to his side.

> And there appeared another wonder in heaven; and behold a great red dragon, having seven heads and ten horns, and seven crowns upon his heads. And his tail drew the third part of the stars of heaven, and did cast them to the earth: and the dragon stood before the woman which was ready to be delivered, for to devour her child as soon as it was born....And the great dragon was cast out, that old serpent, called the Devil, and Satan, which deceiveth the whole world: he was cast out into the earth, and his angels were cast out with him. (Rev 12:1-4,9)

The word translated as "stars" here is almost always identified with angels in the Bible. Notice that the great dragon, as described in verses 3 and 4, is identified in verse 9 as Satan.

God, Who knows all things, knew what Lucifer was doing. After He apparently allowed Lucifer access to His angels (in order to decide which of His angels were truly loyal to Him), He openly proclaimed Lucifer's treachery to all. After proclaiming His Judgment on Lucifer, the loyal angels probably approached God to intervene on Lucifer's behalf. It was not that Lucifer didn't deserve God's Judgment, but that they probably felt that God's Judgment was too severe. Why not simply forgive him, and give him another chance? But God knew Lucifer's heart. He knew that forgiveness would not be coupled by true remorse on Lucifer's part. Lucifer's pride had blackened his heart for eternity. If God were to simply ask if Lucifer wanted forgiveness, Lucifer would simply lie. The other angels, not knowing Lucifer's heart, could easily be deceived by Lucifer's lies. How could God convince His loyal angels that Lucifer did not deserve forgiveness?

To convince His loyal angels, God would Create man! This new creature would be made much lower than the angels so that the angels could invisibly witness God's love for His creatures. But man would have to be in need of God's forgiveness. So God would have to know, beforehand, that man would rebel (i.e., sin) against God's goodness.

The Creation of Mankind

At first, God created everything that man would need. He created a planet (Earth) for man to inhabit. Even though this planet was created to fulfill all of man's needs, God even went so far as to create an especially beautiful garden (Eden) for man to inhabit. He created animals to accompany the man. He went farther when He made His declaration that man was the ruler of this new world.

> **And God said, Let us make man in our image, after our likeness: and let them have dominion over the fish of the sea, and over the fowl of the air, and over the**

GOD'S PLAN

> cattle, and over all the earth, and over every creeping thing that creepeth upon the earth. (Gen 1:26)

> The heaven, even the heavens, are the LORD's: but the earth hath he given to the children of men. (Ps 115:16)

When God makes a declaration, He sticks to it! In order to make the man and the earth interdependent, He actually created the man from the dust of the earth.

> And the LORD God formed man of the dust of the ground, and breathed into his nostrils the breath of life; and man became a living soul. (Gen 2:7)

In fact, the name "Adam" is Hebrew for the earth. Thus in God's declaration, only a man could rule over the earth.

Man was created immortal. So long as the man continued to obey God, man would continue to rule over all the earth immortally. He merely had to obey one simple command.

> And the LORD God commanded the man, saying, Of every tree of the garden thou mayest freely eat: But of the tree of the knowledge of good and evil, thou shalt not eat of it: for in the day that thou eatest thereof thou shalt surely die. (Gen 2:16-17)

The Fall of Man

But God knew that the man (and the woman) would disobey Him. Once again, He did this purposely in order to demonstrate to His loyal angels His love for His creatures. He had devised a complex Plan to redeem man.

When Adam and Eve sinned, they immediately lost their ability to rule over the earth. In fact when God later directed Noah to "Be fruitful, and multiply, and replenish the earth." after the Flood, the directive to rule over the earth is missing.

> And God blessed Noah and his sons, and said unto them, Be fruitful, and multiply, and replenish the earth. (Gen 9:1)

Man and the earth were one. When a person dies, his body returns to the dust of the earth from which he was created.

> In the sweat of thy face shalt thou eat bread, till thou return unto the ground; for out of it wast thou taken: for dust thou art, and unto dust shalt thou return. (Gen 3:19)

After man demonstrated that he could not, or would not, obey God, God deposed him from the throne of the earth. The throne was probably physically located in the Garden of Eden, which God barred Adam from reentering.

> And the LORD God said, Behold, the man is become as one of us, to know good and evil: and now, lest he put forth his hand, and take also of the tree of life, and eat, and live for ever: Therefore the LORD God sent him forth from the garden of Eden, to till the ground from whence he was taken. So he drove out the man; and he placed at the east of the garden of Eden Cherubims, and a flaming sword which turned every way, to keep the way of the tree of life. (Gen 3:22-24)

Once the throne was vacant, Lucifer immediately stepped in and illegally occupied it.

> In whom the god of this world hath blinded the minds of them which believe not, lest the light of the glorious gospel of Christ, who is the image of God, should shine unto them. (2 Cor 4:4)

"The god of this world" refers to Lucifer who, as king of the earth, can pretty much do as he pleases. This situation, however, presents a dilemma for God. How can He redeem mankind to the throne of the earth and, at the same time, overthrow Lucifer from the throne? Lucifer, remember, was perhaps the most powerful angel that God had Created. What *man* could be both powerful enough to overthrow Lucifer and moral enough to justify his seat on the throne? But nothing is impossible for God!

> For with God nothing shall be impossible. (Luke 1:37)

The Protevangelium

After God's Judgment on Adam and Eve, He showed them that He was not finished with mankind. He gave them a mysterious prophecy that explained His Plan to redeem mankind to Him.

> And I will put enmity between thee and the woman, and between thy seed and her seed; it shall bruise thy head, and thou shalt bruise his heel. (Gen 3:15)

This obscure passage is one of the most important passages in the entire Bible. Why? Let's analyze it and see. The passage is addressed to the personality behind the serpent that tempted Eve to sin: Lucifer. The word translated "seed" is in the singular. Hence, Lucifer will produce a singular person to represent him. This person is usually identified by evangelicals as the "antichrist". Why should God allow Lucifer to have a man to represent him? Remember, God wishes to show His loyal angels that Lucifer's perdition is complete. If God allowed Lucifer to rule over the entire world, Lucifer, not able to escape his evil nature, would demonstrate to the whole angelic realm his inability to rule not only the earth but especially over God's Throne. Thus, God's Judgment over Lucifer was not extreme but just. It must be remembered that God has not yet punished Lucifer for his evil. This will come *after* God has proven to His loyal angels that Lucifer's judgment is just.

Interestingly, the other "seed" referred to here is not referred to as God's seed but the woman's. Why a woman's? Anyone who has ever read the Book of Genesis must be struck by the fact that the "begats" (i.e., the lineage of ancient biblical personages) never mentions a woman. Only the men are mentioned. Women's names are only very rarely mentioned until Genesis switches the narrative to concern itself with Abram and his offspring. One would think that since only 8 people were saved through the Flood, the Bible would record the wive's names of Noah, Ham, Shem, and Japheth. But no, only the men's names are recorded. So why does this verse seem to single out a single person as the offspring of a single *woman*?

When Adam and Eve sinned, the fruit of the tree of the knowledge of good and evil apparently did to them as Satan had predicted; they now knew the difference between good and evil.

> **And the eyes of them both were opened, and they knew that they were naked; and they sewed fig leaves together, and made themselves aprons. (Gen 3:7)**

They now knew they were naked! This was the result of eating the fruit. Dr. Henry Morris of the Institute for Creation Research speculates that the fruit had chemical compounds that probably resulted in much more. For one thing, they were now mortal. They were going to die! For another thing, something in the fruit affected the man's reproductive organs. The "sin nature", the rebellion that the two displayed by disobeying God, was passed through the man's seed. Of the "X" and "Y" chromosomes, only the "Y" chromosome was affected. If we remember that the woman's chromosomes are XX and the man's XY, only the man's was affected.

> **For since by man came death, by man came also the resurrection of the dead. For as in Adam all die, even so in Christ shall all be made alive. (1 Cor 15:21-22)**

If the "sin nature" is passed only through the man, the woman's seed is clean. This is important. In order for a human being to escape the "sin nature", he, or she, must be born of a virgin! Such a person would not be compelled to sin as the rest of us are.

This scenario actually reveals the beauty and perfection of God's Plan for the redemption of mankind. If God were to be born into human flesh via a virgin, He would not have the "sin nature" even though physically He's a man but spiritually He's God. This explains why God's "seed" must be born of a woman – a virgin! God cannot "sin"; that is, He cannot rebel against Himself. Therefore, He would satisfy the moral requirements that Adam failed to as "king of the Earth". Because God now has a human body, He would also satisfy the requirement that only a *man* could be "king of the Earth" as demanded by God's own declaration. Remember, Jesus' favorite title for Himself was "the Son of Man".

> And I saw in the right hand of him that sat on the throne a book written within and on the backside, sealed with seven seals. And I saw a strong angel proclaiming with a loud voice, Who is worthy to open the book, and to loose the seals thereof? And no man in heaven, nor in earth, neither under the earth, was able to open the book, neither to look thereon. And I wept much, because no man was found worthy to open and to read the book, neither to look thereon. And one of the elders saith unto me, Weep not: behold, the Lion of the tribe of Juda, the Root of David, hath prevailed to open the book, and to loose the seven seals thereof. And I beheld, and, lo, in the midst of the throne and of the four beasts, and in the midst of the elders, stood a Lamb as it had been slain, having seven horns and seven eyes, which are the seven Spirits of God sent forth into all the earth. And he came and took the book out of the right hand of him that sat upon the throne. And when he had taken the book, the four beasts and four *and* twenty elders fell down before the Lamb, having every one of them harps, and golden vials full of odours, which are the prayers of saints. And they sung a new song, saying, Thou art worthy to take the book, and to open the seals thereof: for thou wast slain, and hast redeemed us to God by thy blood out of every kindred, and tongue, and people, and nation; And hast made us

> **unto our God kings and priests: and we shall reign on the earth. (Rev 5:1-10)**

This passage should convince anyone that Jesus, as "the Lion of the tribe of Juda", "the Root of David", and "a Lamb as it had been slain", is the only *man* worthy enough to open the book. What is this book? It's obviously the certificate of sovereignty over the earth as witnessed by the last verse where it's said "we shall reign on the earth". Thirdly since no other angel, or man, has the power to wrest the earth's throne from Lucifer, only God can.

What a verse! What a Plan! In fact, this verse (Gen. 3:15) has been dubbed "The Protevangelium", or first Gospel, by true, biblical scholars. This verse, furthermore, has been inscribed in the signs of the zodiac. See <u>The Gospel in the Stars</u> by Joseph Seiss for verification of this.

The Redemption of Mankind

There is, however, one thing this verse fails to explain. How could God forgive sinful man for his transgressions and still satisfy His Justice? This part of the Plan is just as beautiful and perfect as that revealed in the Protevangelium.

Jesus was the only person ever documented to be born of a virgin.

> **Therefore the Lord himself shall give you a sign; Behold, a virgin shall conceive, and bear a son, and shall call his name Immanuel. (Isa 7:14)**

The name "Immanuel" means "God with us". Admittedly, this does not sound like Jesus. The *meaning* is what's important here. Jesus is the English translation of the Greek name Iesous (there was no letter "J" in the Greek). Furthermore, the name "Iesous" was the Greek translation of the Hebrew name of "Joshua", or "Yeshua". Joshua means "the Lord is salvation". Hence, "Immanuel" and "Jesus" are basically synonymous. Because Jesus was the only person to have ever been born of a virgin, this prophecy identifies

Him as God! Thus, Jesus fills the requirements set forth in The Protevangelium as the offspring of the woman. What makes the birth of Jesus by a virgin even more miraculous is the scientific fact that parthenogenesis (i.e. virgin birth) when witnessed in the more "primitive" animal species always corresponds in the offspring having all the DNA characteristics of the mother (since there is no father). Jesus not only did not have these characteristics (i.e., of only His mother's DNA), but He was born of the opposite gender (i.e., He's a male).

Since Jesus was born "sinless", He could pay the "sin" penalty for mankind as a substitute. The Jews were required to employ a whole system of blood sacrifices in order to "pay" for their sins. But these sacrifices were never really meant to pay for their sins but to look forward to Jesus' perfect sacrifice.

> For it is not possible that the blood of bulls and of goats should take away sins. (Heb 10:4)

This He did by dying on the cross! This is what The Protevangelium describes as Satan "striking the woman's seed's heel". Lucifer's strike at the seed's heel would not be permanent, but the woman's seed's crushing of the head of the serpent's offspring would be. Therefore, Jesus would eventually emerge victorious. The serpent's offspring, or the antichrist, will be cast into a lake of fire along with Lucifer for eternity.

> And the devil that deceived them was cast into the lake of fire and brimstone, where the beast and the false prophet *are,* and shall be tormented day and night for ever and ever. (Rev 20:10)

Now that Jesus paid the sin penalty for man, what importance can we attach to it? God could now redeem mankind to Himself one sinner at a time. Only those sinners who, unlike Lucifer, showed true repentance for their sin nature (not their sins because these are a result of our nature) can be redeemed. Those who reject Jesus' kind offer of salvation will not be forced to accept Him. This is much the same situation as the loyal and fallen angels. This forgiveness is truly by the grace of God. This situation is closely witnessed by God's loyal angels.

> Of which salvation the prophets have inquired and searched diligently, who prophesied of the grace that should come unto you: Searching what, or what manner of time the Spirit of Christ which was in them did signify, when it testified beforehand the sufferings of Christ, and the glory that should follow. Unto whom it was revealed, that not unto themselves, but unto us they did minister the things, which are now reported unto you by them that have preached the gospel unto you with the Holy Ghost sent down from heaven; which things the angels desire to look into. (1 Pet 1:10-12)

The Bible, furthermore, hints at the idea that salvation is offered to all.

> For we know that the whole creation groaneth and travaileth in pain together until now. (Rom 8:22)

Why would God's whole Creation be in pain if only Adam's and Eve's sin was in view. Their sin, it seems likely, would only affect the earth and mankind. Obviously, the rebellion of Lucifer and the fallen angels can also be forgiven by simply partaking of God's salvation.

God wishes us to be faithful. This is the only requirement for forgiveness.

> For by grace are ye saved through faith; and that not of yourselves: it is the gift of God: Not of works, lest any man should boast. (Eph 2:8-9)

Angels, who can witness this, will see and understand that God gives us His wonderful forgiveness freely. But more so, He shows His love to all of His creatures by sacrificing His Son on the cross in the most horrible way imaginable in order to do so. No matter how rebellious or sinful we've been, God loves us so much that He's willing to do this for us.

> For scarcely for a righteous man will one die: yet peradventure for a good man some would even dare to die. But God commendeth his love toward us, in that, while we were yet sinners, Christ died for us. (Rom 5:7-8)

This is extremely remarkable! Christ died for us even though we were His enemies! This demonstrates the lengths that God is willing to go to save His creatures out of His love for them. The angels must be very impressed indeed!

Eternal Salvation

Furthermore, this salvation is eternal.

> These things have I written unto you that believe on the name of the Son of God; that ye may know that ye have eternal life, and that ye may believe on the name of the Son of God. (I Jn 5:13)

> For I am persuaded, that neither death, nor life, nor angels, nor principalities, nor powers, nor things present, nor things to come, Nor height, nor depth, nor any other creature, shall be able to separate us from the love of God, which is in Christ Jesus our Lord. (Rom 8:38-39)

> For the gifts and calling of God are without repentance. (Rom 11:29)

If you can *know* that you have eternal life, it means that you can obtain eternal life during your current lifetime. There's no need to wait until death. There's no weighing of good deeds versus sinful acts. In fact, it is a *gift* from God! There's absolutely nothing we can do other than to ask God for His unspeakable gift. This is the good news of the Christian Gospel. It's a biblical doctrine known as *eternal security*. Let's examine this doctrine.

The Greek word translated as "eternal" in I John 5:13 is "aionios" and means perpetual, everlasting, or forever. This cinches the translation. In Romans 8:38-39, the Apostle Paul indicates that nothing that he knows of can break this security. And in Romans 11:29 Paul tells us that once God calls us and grants us His gifts, He never rescinds them. This is very strong evidence that the doctrine of eternal security is true.

There are those who argue that Paul's statement in Romans 8:38-39 doesn't include us. This, they further argue, means that, even though no outside forces can affect our salvation, we can lose it ourselves. Furthermore, the doctrine of eternal security makes no provisions for future sinfulness. That is, eternal security allows us to continue in our previous state of sin without penalty.

These arguments are neither biblical, logical, nor consistent with the Protevangelium. Firstly, they are not biblical.

> What shall we say then? Shall we continue in sin, that grace may abound? God forbid. How shall we, that are dead to sin, live any longer therein? Know ye not, that so many of us as were baptized into Jesus Christ were baptized into his death? Therefore we are buried with him by baptism into death: that like as Christ was raised up from the dead by the glory of the Father, even so we also should walk in newness of life. For if we have been planted together in the likeness of his death, we shall be also in the likeness of his resurrection: Knowing this, that our old man is crucified with him, that the body of sin might be destroyed, that henceforth we should not serve sin. For he that is dead is freed from sin. Now if we be dead with Christ, we believe that we shall also live with him: Knowing that Christ being raised from the dead dieth no more; death hath no more dominion over him. For in that he died, he died unto sin once: but in

GOD'S PLAN

> that he liveth, he liveth unto God. Likewise reckon ye also yourselves to be dead indeed unto sin, but alive unto God through Jesus Christ our Lord. Let not sin therefore reign in your mortal body, that ye should obey it in the lusts thereof. Neither yield ye your members as instruments of unrighteousness unto sin: but yield yourselves unto God, as those that are alive from the dead, and your members as instruments of righteousness unto God. For sin shall not have dominion over you: for ye are not under the law, but under grace. What then? shall we sin, because we are not under the law, but under grace? God forbid. Know ye not, that to whom ye yield yourselves servants to obey, his servants ye are to whom ye obey; whether of sin unto death, or of obedience unto righteousness? But God be thanked, that ye were the servants of sin, but ye have obeyed from the heart that form of doctrine which was delivered you. Being then made free from sin, ye became the servants of righteousness. I speak after the manner of men because of the infirmity of your flesh: for as ye have yielded your members servants to uncleanness and to iniquity unto iniquity; even so now yield your members servants to righteousness unto holiness. For when ye were the servants of sin, ye were free from righteousness. What fruit had ye then in those things whereof ye are now ashamed? for the end of those things is death. But now being made free from sin, and become servants to God, ye have your fruit unto holiness, and the end everlasting life. For the wages of sin is death; but the gift of God is eternal life through Jesus Christ our Lord. (Rom 6:1-23)

This is the entirety of Romans Chapter 6 and Paul's complete argument for eternal security. Notice that Paul continually refers to the death of sin in our lives. This is consistent with the Protevangelium. What Paul is referring to is the death of our sin *natures*. Even though we will continue to sin so long as we remain in our presently corrupted bodies, to God our bodies have died, and we await a resurrection of new, uncorrupted bodies.

> So also is the resurrection of the dead. It is sown in corruption; it is raised in incorruption: It is sown in dishonour; it is raised in glory: it is sown in weakness; it is raised in power: It is sown a natural body; it is raised a spiritual body. There is a natural body, and there is a spiritual body. (1 Cor 15:42-44)

Furthermore, the arguments just presented against the doctrine of eternal security confuse salvation with rewards.

> Now he that planteth and he that watereth are one: and every man shall receive his own reward according to his own labour. For we are labourers together with God: ye are God's husbandry, ye are God's building. According to the grace of God which is given unto me, as a wise masterbuilder, I have laid the foundation, and another buildeth thereon. But let every man take heed how he buildeth thereupon.
>
> For other foundation can no man lay than that is laid, which is Jesus Christ. Now if any man build upon this foundation gold, silver, precious stones, wood, hay, stubble; Every man's work shall be made manifest: for the day shall declare it, because it shall be revealed by fire; and the fire shall try every man's work of what sort it is. If any man's work abide which he hath built thereupon, he shall receive a reward. If any man's work shall be burned, he shall suffer loss: but he himself shall be saved; yet so as by fire. (1 Cor 3:8-15)

Notice the last verse that states that someone who gathers no rewards for himself will suffer loss but still remain saved!

The last counter argument that we will submit is based on the Greek word "aionios" which we've already translated as "eternal". God does not save us by degrees. It is a once-for-all declaration of salvation. The scriptural words for salvation and righteousness are synonymous. Righteousness is simply the opposite concept of "wrongness" or sinlessness. That is, someone who is declared righteous has no further need of salvation since they've never done any "wrong"; they are "perfect".

> And he believed in the LORD; and he counted it to him for righteousness. (Gen 15:6)

This verse records the very moment of Abram's (i.e., Abraham's) salvation. The accreditation of righteousness to Abram means that God declared Abram righteous from then on. Paul uses this very same argument in Romans.

> For what saith the scripture? Abraham believed God, and it was counted unto him for righteousness. (Rom 4:3)

Remember, God's gift and call are irrevocable. So if we are saved for eternity once God declares us as righteous, our eternal security is established or else eternity does not mean forever – it means temporary. But we have just seen that "aionios" *does* mean forever! Thus, we must conclude that the doctrine of eternal security is validated.

We must also remember that Jesus' sacrifice was both perfect and complete because God never does anything imperfectly or half way. To pray to anyone other than Jesus demonstrates that we really don't accredit Him for this. Or to count on satisfying some observance or ritual also means that we don't trust Him entirely for our salvation. Many of us trust in our own works. Paul argues poignantly against this. He says that if we could work (i.e., obey God) for our salvation, then God owes us the wages we've earned for our work. But no one can perfectly obey God because of our sin natures.

> Now to him that worketh is the reward not reckoned of grace, but of debt. But to him that worketh not, but believeth on him that justifieth the ungodly, his faith is counted for righteousness. (Rom 4:4-5)

> For by grace are ye saved through faith; and that not of yourselves: it is the gift of God: Not of works, lest any man should boast. (Eph 2:8-9)

> I do not frustrate the grace of God: for if righteousness come by the law, then Christ is dead in vain. (Gal 2:21)

This point cannot be emphasized enough! Remember, God's *gift* of salvation is offered by His own grace (i.e., love). If anyone could perfectly obey the law (i.e., God's commandments), then Jesus was foolish to die for us in such a horrible way.

> For there is one God, and one mediator between God and men, the man Christ Jesus; (1 Tim 2:5)

This verse should cinch to Whom we should rely upon, period! There is no one else or nothing else. All of our prayers should be directed to Whom we place our trust in salvation. Our confessions, our desires, and our petitions should be directed to Him and not ourselves or our works. Remember, salvation is based upon a personal relationship between ourselves and our Lord because He, and He alone, paid the ransom price for our souls.

This verse also reflects the simplicity, completeness, and perfection of God's Plan. The combination of man and God in Jesus allows us to petition the one sinless man who ever lived, "the *man* Christ Jesus", for forgiveness of our sins. Because Jesus is both man and God, the human side of Jesus, who can identify with our weaknesses, can converse directly with His God-side and forgive our sins. What a perfect Plan that's so simple and yet so difficult to accomplish! Only the God of the Bible could ever have conceived of such a Plan and bring it to fruition.

GOD'S PLAN

There's only one question that we, as sinful human beings, can raise. Why should we have to suffer for Adam's sin? After all, we didn't *choose* to disobey God. Our sinful natures are an unfair imposition on us. But if my model of God's Plan is correct, we were Created for this purpose. The simple Plan of Salvation requires us to do almost nothing for ourselves other than faith. And if someone really wishes to address fairness, let's take a look at what our salvation cost Jesus. He died in the most agonizingly, shameful, and public way possible just so we could be saved in the first place. This, then, should answer *any* questions of unfairness.

Sanctification

Before we completely leave the subject of eternal security, I would feel remiss for not bringing up the doctrine of *sanctification*. Sanctification is different than salvation. Salvation is an act; it is a declaration of righteousness from God. Sanctification is a lifelong process; we must learn to become more like Jesus after we've been saved. We have already read the Scriptural reference for rewards. This is sanctification. What does sanctification mean? It comes from the Greek word "hagios", which means holy. It also means "separate" (i.e., the noun "separate"). Thus, we are to be separated unto God. The word "sanctified", I believe, was shortened to "sanct" and then to "saint". This is unfortunate because everyone who has been saved is a "saint". This happens because separation unto God can have multiple meanings (viz. those who are saved are separated unto God). The kind of sanctification I'm trying to explain here is our lifelong walk with Christ. Allow me to explain this doctrine of sanctification since it is so crucial to the Christian's life.

Sanctification bridges the gulf between Arminianism, or Wesleyanism, and Calvinism. In the Arminian doctrine, saints can lose their salvation if they don't persevere in their walk with Christ to the end. By contrast, Calvinists believe in eternal security but also maintain that those who don't persevere were probably not saved to begin with. Sanctification solves this problem. It clearly teaches eternal security, but the Bible also clearly identifies so-called "carnal" Christians who don't persevere until the end of life. Sanctification calls for all Christians to persevere in order to attain to rewards.

Anyone who has read the New Testament must be struck by the fact that there are numerous passages that allude to sin and the inheritance of the kingdom of God. I'll repeat here just one such passage.

> Now the works of the flesh are manifest, which are *these;* Adultery, fornication, uncleanness, lasciviousness, Idolatry, witchcraft, hatred, variance, emulations, wrath, strife, seditions, heresies, Envyings, murders, drunkenness, revellings, and such like: of the which I tell you before, as I have also told *you* in time past, that they which do such things shall not inherit the kingdom of God. (Gal. 5:19-21)

Most of these sins such as idolatry, witchcraft, murders, etc. we needn't worry about. But some of them such as adultery, hatred, wrath, envyings, and drunkenness have touched at least a few of us – even after we've been "saved". As I've already mentioned, salvation does not keep us from sinning. This is the job of sanctification. Once we've been saved, we're assured of not going to Hell regardless of the way we behave. But notice that the passage says nothing of salvation; it speaks of inheriting the kingdom of God. Jesus not only wants us to be saved, but He also wants us to reign with Him in His future kingdom.

Once again, let's use Scripture to identify this doctrine.

> For by grace are ye saved through faith; and that not of yourselves: *it is* the gift of God: Not of works, lest any man should boast. For we are his workmanship, created in Christ Jesus unto good works, which God hath before ordained that we should walk in them. (Eph 2:8-10)

The first two verses of this reference have already been alluded to in order to highlight God's Plan of Salvation. Please notice that these two verses end in a period. In English grammar, this means that the thought is complete. The next sentence, which begins with the word "for", is a completely new thought. Once we've been saved, it is God's job ("his workmanship") to perfect us if we'll let Him. This requires submission on our part.

Sanctification is, basically, a three step process.

> And now abideth faith, hope, charity, these three; but the greatest of these *is* charity. (1 Cor 13:13)

Paul says that we must grow from faith (our initial requirement for Salvation) to hope and then from hope to charity. The word translated as "charity" is the Greek word "agape" and means true, sacrificial love. I believe I've identified the three chapters in the Bible that underscore what each of these steps describe: faith is Hebrews Chapter 11; hope is 1 Corinthians Chapter 15; and love is 1 Corinthians Chapter 13.

In the book of 1 John, John further describes these steps.

> I write unto you, little children, because your sins are forgiven you for his name's sake. I write unto you, fathers, because ye have known him *that is* from the beginning. I write unto you, young men, because ye have overcome the wicked one. I write unto you, little children, because ye have known the Father. I have written unto you, fathers, because ye have known him *that is* from the beginning. I have written unto you, young men, because ye are strong, and the word of God abideth in you, and ye have overcome the wicked one. (1 John 2:12-14)

Please notice that John addresses three groups of people. They're in the natural progression of age that our bodies undergo as time passes: "little children", "young men", and "fathers". The "little children" have had their sins forgiven and have known the father (i.e., salvation). Since salvation requires faith, these "little children" have been saved but have not yet grown in their walk with the Lord. The "young men" have the Word of God abiding in them and have overcome Satan (is this hope?). The "fathers" have known Him Who is from the beginning (love).

> Beloved, now are we the sons of God, and it doth not yet appear what we shall be: but we know that, when he shall appear, we shall be like him; for we shall see him as he is. And every man that hath this hope in him purifieth himself, even as he is pure. (1 John 3:2-3)

This is the hope – that we shall be like Him.

> And we have known and believed the love that God hath to us. God is love; and he that dwelleth in love dwelleth in God, and God in him. Herein is our love made perfect, that we may have boldness in the day of judgment: because as he is, so are we in this world. There is no fear in love; but perfect love casteth out fear: because fear hath torment. He that feareth is not made perfect in love. We love him, because he first loved us. (1 John 4:16-19)

This is love – that we know Him and fear is cast out.

What I'm trying to say here is that these three steps are crucial in our day-to-day Christian walk. I do not personally believe that this three-step process of sanctification can be skipped over. For example, I don't believe that any of us can skip over from faith to love without going through the process of hope. I also believe that anyone who claims to do so is deceiving themselves.

As God tries to perfect us, He will throw some very hard tests our way so that we can learn.

> And ye have forgotten the exhortation which speaketh unto you as unto children, My son, despise not thou

> the chastening of the Lord, nor faint when thou art rebuked of him: For whom the Lord loveth he chasteneth, and scourgeth every son whom he receiveth. If ye endure chastening, God dealeth with you as with sons; for what son is he whom the father chasteneth not? But if ye be without chastisement, whereof all are partakers, then are ye bastards, and not sons. (Heb 12:5-8)

He does this so that we're not merely saved but that we can reign with Him. This He desires most of all. Those who pass all the tests are called, in the Greek, the "metachoi". This word is almost invariably translated as "overcomer" in the King James Version.

As Joseph Dillow in The Reign of the Servant Kings and Chuck and Nancy Missler in The Kingdom, Power, and Glory point out, this topic is almost never discussed in Christian Churches. In both books, Jesus' parables about "outer darkness" and "the weeping and gnashing of teeth" are treated in an unfamiliar way.

> And when the king came in to see the guests, he saw there a man which had not on a wedding garment: And he saith unto him, Friend, how camest thou in hither not having a wedding garment? And he was speechless. Then said the king to the servants, Bind him hand and foot, and take him away, and cast *him* into outer darkness; there shall be weeping and gnashing of teeth. For many are called, but few *are* chosen. (Mat 22:11-14)

According to both books, these "guests" are saved! The "outer darkness" referred to here is *not* hell. Rather, it is the outer courtyard of the millennial temple. The inner court of the temple will be constantly lit by God's light. The outer court will not. Both, however, will be part of the temple complex in Jesus' reign. The phrase "weeping and gnashing of teeth" is a particular Jewish phrase that literally indicates frustration. The Christian will be frustrated with himself for not taking advantage of events that he could have that would have resulted in the rewards to allow him into the inner temple and become an "overcomer".

Chuck and Nancy Missler explain sanctification in terms of how it affects our tripartite being: body, soul, and spirit. Our bodies contain the sin nature. Because of this, they are irredeemable in their present state. They will, however, be modified on the day of resurrection and given back to us.

> Jesus answered and said unto him, Verily, verily, I say unto thee, Except a man be born again, he cannot see the kingdom of God. Nicodemus saith unto him, How can a man be born when he is old? can he enter the second time into his mother's womb, and be born? Jesus answered, Verily, verily, I say unto thee, Except a man be born of water and *of* the Spirit, he cannot enter into the kingdom of God. That which is born of the flesh is flesh; and that which is born of the Spirit is spirit. Marvel not that I said unto thee, Ye must be born again. (John 3:3-7)

This is the passage that Christians refer to for being "born again". Since none of us has, as yet, entered God's Kingdom, the phrase "born again" refers to the absolute belief in our resurrection. The allusion to "flesh" here refers to human flesh. That is, we cannot enter the kingdom of God in these corruptible bodies.

The spirit is that part of us that includes our intellect. This is the part of us that is immediately saved at God's declaration of salvation. Thus, our modified bodies and our spirits will enter in to God's eternal salvation.It is our souls, the seat of our emotions, that must be sanctified.

As we submit our wills to Him in faith, hope, and love, He modifies us so that we may participate in His reign over the earth. We must remember that salvation doesn't require us to love Him; only faith is required. But if we do love Him, the Bible promises us a lot.

> **But as it is written, Eye hath not seen, nor ear heard, neither have entered into the heart of man, the things which God hath prepared for them that love him. (1 Cor 2:9)**

The Two Advents

Now let's return to the Protevangelium and God's Plan. Christ's atonement for our sin natures was the part of the Protevangelium that dealt with the serpent's seed that struck the heel of the woman's seed. This means that the serpent's seed will cause injury to the woman's seed, but it won't be permanent. This is attested to historically with the Resurrection of Jesus. Jesus is still alive and well! From this point on, we'll consider the prophecy of the woman's seed crushing the head of the serpent's seed.

Remember that the serpent referred to in the Protevangelium is actually referring to the power behind the serpent: Lucifer. As was stated earlier, God must allow Lucifer and his minions of dark angels to rule completely over mankind on planet earth to demonstrate to His angels that he is not worthy of such rulership. Lucifer will rule via his counterpart: the man biblical scholars refer to as the antichrist. Jesus' mission and the antichrist's reign together comprise one week: seven years split down the middle or 3½ years each. This timing, and Lucifer's rule, will be covered more exhaustively later. The occurrence that will cut the antichrist's reign down is Jesus' Second Advent. He will kill the antichrist (the serpent's seed) and throw the antichrist's spirit, Lucifer, and his fallen angels into hell for 1,000 years.

How do we know this? The ancient, Jewish scholars, when studying the Protevangelium and other Scriptures, concluded that there would be one coming of two Messiahs. One of them would be a suffering Messiah, and the other would be a conquering Messiah. From their own history and the Bible, they named the suffering Messiah "Messiah ben Joseph" after Joseph's sufferings. The other Messiah they named after Israel's greatest king, "Messiah ben David". He would be the conquering Messiah. The Hebrew word "ben" means "son of". What confused the Pharisees and the other Jews during the time of Jesus was that they hadn't reckoned on the possibility of two comings of the same Messiah.

Had they studied their own Bibles more carefully, they would have realized that God had planned on this second scenario from the beginning.

> Then shall we know, if we follow on to know the LORD: his going forth is prepared as the morning; and he shall come unto us as the rain, as the latter and former rain unto the earth. (Hosea 6:3)

> Be patient therefore, brethren, unto the coming of the Lord. Behold, the husbandman waiteth for the precious fruit of the earth, and hath long patience for it, until he receive the early and latter rain. (James 5:7)

This theme of the Lord's coming as the early and latter rains is repeated in many places in the Bible. Now the only way that the Lord could come as the early and latter rains would be that He would have to come twice! Furthermore, His two comings would coincide with these two harvest seasons in Israel: the autumn and the spring.

Jewish Feasts

God further gave the Jewish people 7 observances that the Jews were commanded to observe. These feasts were more than simple holidays because they pointed to certain, important events in Jesus' overall ministry. These feasts are covered in Leviticus Chapter 23. Four of them occur at the time of the spring harvest. They are Passover, Bitter Herbs, First Fruits, and Pentecost. The last three occur at the time of the autumn harvest. They are Rosh Hashanah (first of the year), Yom Kippur (Day of Atonement), and Shavuot (Tabernacles). A study of the first four feasts reveals that something important occurred in God's Plan centered on Jesus' First Advent. Jesus was crucified on Passover. Bitter Herbs

GOD'S PLAN

was observed while Jesus lay dead and buried. First Fruits was celebrated on the day of Jesus' Resurrection. And the Holy Spirit fell on the disciples on the day of Pentecost and the founding of Christ's Church.

It is expected that, just as the spring feasts represented something important in God's Plan, the autumn feasts will be just as important. For example, many biblical scholars believe that the Rapture of the Church (more on this later) will occur on Rosh Hashanah. An excellent book on this subject is Joseph Good's Rosh Hashanah and the Messianic Kingdom to Come. Many also believe that Yom Kippur will host Jesus' Second Advent.

The Second Advent

At the Second Advent of Christ, Jesus will return and claim that which is rightfully His: the throne of the earth. Of course, Lucifer, the fallen angels, and unregenerate man will oppose Him. All hell will break loose on the earth. Jesus and His Church, however, will overcome them all and establish His throne of righteousness. During this time, mankind will be free from the influences of Lucifer but still, once again, fail God's test. Those who do pass God's test will be admitted into God's family and the redemption of mankind will be completed.

Dispensationalism

God, the careful Planner that He is, must obviously have constructed His Plan down to very precise specifics. One of these is based on time periods. One of the most popular "theories" held by biblical scholars is called *dispensationalism* or *Chiliasm*. This "theory" holds that God decided, beforehand, that, just as it took 7 days to Create the world, He would allow 7 "days" for the redemption of fallen mankind. Each of these "days" would begin with God dispensing a new revelation to mankind. God would allow mankind to use this new revelation to prove to Him and the angelic realm that mankind was worthy of redemption. Each new revelation would be abused by mankind and, hence, incur

God's punishment. Each of these "days", also called *ages*, would last approximately 1,000 years and end in Judgment. Again, there would be 7 of them.

Let us attempt, now, to justify this theory. According to a tradition supposedly attributed to the Prophet Elijah, just as God took 6 days to Create the Earth and rested on the seventh, He will restore all things in 6,000 years and rest for the last 1,000 years. Just as Jews observe the seventh day of the week as the Sabbath, the seventh millennium is known as the Sabbath millennium. From no less a secular source as Edward Gibbon, we read in Chapter 15 of his The Decline and Fall of the Roman Empire:

> The ancient and popular doctrine of the Millennium was intimately connected with the second coming of Christ. As the works of the creation had been finished in six days, their duration in their present state, according to a tradition which was attributed to the prophet Elijah, was fixed to six thousand years. By the same analogy it was inferred that this long period of labour and contention, which was now almost elapsed, would be succeeded by a joyful Sabbath of a thousand years; and that Christ, with the triumphant band of the saints and the elect *who had escaped death*, or who had been miraculously revived, would reign upon earth till the time appointed for the last and general resurrection.

I have purposely italicized the words "who had escaped death" for purposes that will become clear much later in our study. For now, let us merely file this information away for future use.

As further support, we refer to an extra-biblical document known as Barnabbas and supposedly attributed to the well-known fellow traveler with the Apostle Paul by the same name. At one time, this book was considered for inclusion into the New Testament because it was known that the book was read in the early church meetings.

> And even in the beginning of the creation he makes mention of the sabbath. And God made in six days the works of his hands; and he finished them on the seventh day, and he rested the seventh day, and sanctified it. Consider, my children, what that signifies, he finished them in six days. The meaning of it is this; that in six thousand years the Lord God will bring all things to an end. For with him one day is a thousand years; as himself testifieth, saying, Behold this day shall be as a thousand years. Therefore, children, in six days, that is, in six thousand years, shall all things be accomplished. And what is that he saith, And he rested the seventh day: he meaneth this; that when his Son shall come, and abolish the season of the Wicked One, and judge the ungodly; and shall change the sun and the moon, and the stars; then he shall gloriously rest in that seventh day. (Barnabbas 8:3-6)

The biblical authority for this "theory" rests on two passages of Scripture:

> But, beloved, be not ignorant of this one thing, that one day is with the Lord as a thousand years, and a thousand years as one day. (2 Pet 3:8)

> For a thousand years in thy sight are but as yesterday when it is past, and as a watch in the night. (Ps 90:4)

As we can see, the first Christians believed the Dispensational Theory 2,000 years ago. It connects each of the six days of Creation with a thousand-year duration. Each of these thousand-year periods, or ages, begins with God revealing something new to mankind in order to allow mankind to reconcile for his rebellion and ends in God's Judgment for mankind's abuse of God's new Revelation.

Without a proper understanding of this theory and grounding in this doctrine, it is impossible to truly and to thoroughly understand the tenet of Scripture. It is important to realize that some of the Dispensations are clearly marked and defined from beginning to end; some are not. Furthermore, the thousand-year duration (with the sole exception of the Sabbath Age, or Christ's Reign on Earth) is a general guideline and not to be followed strictly. The Church Age, for example, is at least a two thousand-year age.

There are, unfortunately, several opinions held by biblical scholars as to the identification of the dispensations, their beginnings, and their endings. The Dispensational Theory espoused and popularized by C. I. Scofield in his commentary Bible known as the Scofield Study Bible is the one to which we shall adhere. These ages are as follows.

I. Innocence

II. Conscience

III. Government

IV. Promise

V. Law

VI. Grace or the Church

VII. The Kingdom or the Millennium

As mentioned at the beginning of this chapter, God's Plan, as just presented, is merely a "model" even though about 95% of it is biblically based. It should be used as a means for understanding the Scriptures. If it in any way diverges from its intended purpose, it should either be modified or summarily rejected. If it only diverges moderately, perhaps a slight adjustment is in order. If it diverges wildly, it should be rejected in its entirety.

This Plan, in my mind, helps to clear up many objections to biblical truth. God's overall Plan of Redemption and dispensationalism, if

Chapter 4

DISPENSATION 1: INNOCENCE

The first dispensation is called the Age of Innocence by Dr. Scofield. It is called this because man was Created and placed in a perfect, paradisiacal environment protected and watched over by God. Man was given only the information God decided was in his best interests to protect him from the knowledge of good and evil. As such, man had to completely trust in God to watch over and protect him. The Tree of the Knowledge of Good and Evil was placed in the garden to give man the "opportunity" to revoke God's protective umbrella and to place man's responsibility for protection from evil upon himself. Man merely had to eat of the fruit of this tree to replace his innocence with this forbidden knowledge. God had warned man what would befall him if he decided to partake of this fruit: his immortality would end (since he was protected by God); he would drive a wedge between himself and God (since he rejected God's protection); and he would be helpless against the more powerful forces of evil which he, beforehand, could not know existed in the universe.

God originally gave man everything he could possibly dream of. The man was Created as the sovereign (or, ruler) over all he surveyed; the Earth was his. God placed the stewardship of the Earth in man's hands so long as he demonstrated the perfect character necessary to maintain his position. In God's economy, the Earth was made for man; and the man was made for the Earth. God's act of creating man from the dust of the Earth, therefore, was more than a mere symbolic act. The man and the Earth were connected physically. He placed beautiful animals in the garden for man's edification. He placed all kinds of plants in the garden for the man's sustenance. He placed the Tree of Life in the garden to allow the man to eat of its fruits and live eternally. He also Created a woman as a companion and "help-meet" for the man.

When man disobeyed God, he revoked his privilege to continue to rule over the earth because he no longer retained the moral capacity to do so. Furthermore, the revocation of God's protection left man completely helpless against the more powerful forces of evil that existed in the universe: Satan and his minions. Man no longer had the perfect character required by God to maintain his stewardship over the Earth. His dominion was taken from him, and Satan stepped into the breach. This new, helpless state of affairs allowed Satan to assume rulership over the earth. This is the status of the world today.

The Age of Innocence began with the Creation of the man and ended with God's Judgment over man's fall. This period is covered by Genesis Chapters 1 through 3. In between, many provocative and important points of interest occurred. We shall now look at some of these.

Creation of the World

That God Created the world cannot be disputed if the Bible is sincerely taken as inspired and literal. This begins in Genesis 1:1:

> **In the beginning God created the heaven and the earth. (Gen 1:1)**

Let us carefully analyze this opening statement of the Bible. Firstly, the Bible openly mentions God in its very beginning; it does not go into carefully contrived, philosophical statements about His existence, His character, His attributes, etc. Thus, the Bible begins, without apology, declaring all these things as something mankind already knows. Other parts of the Bible declare this:

> The fool hath said in his heart, There is no God. They are corrupt, they have done abominable works, there is none that doeth good. (Ps 14:1)

Please take special notice of this quotation. The fool has said this in his *heart* - not his mind! Since the heart is taken as the centerpiece of emotion in biblical literature, fools reject the existence of God because they are emotionally set against Him. Furthermore:

> For the wrath of God is revealed from heaven against all ungodliness and unrighteousness of men, who hold the truth in unrighteousness; Because that which may be known of God is manifest in them; for God hath shewed it unto them. For the invisible things of him from the creation of the world are clearly seen, being understood by the things that are made, even his eternal power and Godhead; so that they are without excuse: Because that, when they knew God, they glorified him not as God, neither were thankful; but became vain in their imaginations, and their foolish heart was darkened. Professing themselves to be wise, they became fools, And changed the glory of the uncorruptible God into an image made like to corruptible man, and to birds, and fourfooted beasts, and creeping things. (Rom 1:18-23)

These verses clearly state that all men once knew about God from Noah and his sons. Also, their ignorance of God is inexcusable since God's Creation and Sovereignty are visible to all.

Another thing that we observe from Genesis 1:1 is contained in the phrase "In the beginning". We must ask, the beginning of what? According to most biblical scholars, this phrase refers to time. When God Created the heavens and the earth, He foreknew of mankind's fall and began His Plan for the redemption (i.e., reconciliation) of mankind. This act started the countdown as day

1 of 7,000 years as we have delineated in our quote from the Book of Barnabbas. Bishop Ussher, in his famous chronology, believes this act was performed in the year 4004 B.C. He came to this conclusion by basing his count on an archaeologically established date and then counting through the generations, as recorded in the Old Testament, backwards. He made one paramount assumption: that the ages of the people, as recorded in the Old Testament, contain no gaps. It is normal, in biblical literature, for one man to be recorded as the father of another man although there may have been several generations skipped over. Based on this assumption, other, prominent biblical scholars have counted backwards over differing, established archaeological dates and have come up with similar conclusions. This, then, is the year we shall use. Furthermore, the Jews, on their civil calendar, mark the date of Creation as Tishri 1. This is the September to early October timeframe on our calendars. The movement of the date of Tishri 1 with our calendar is because the Jewish calendar was based on the lunar cycles rather than our solar cycles. Because of this, the Jewish calendar year is 360 days (30*12) in duration. Tishri 1 is also the celebration of the Jewish Feast of Trumpets, Rosh Hashanah, or Jewish New Year. This date has been calculated as October 23rd. As of today, the Jewish calendar is approximately in the year 5770. Since some 200 to 250 years were not recorded on their calendar because of some unpopular Persian kings (see George Foot Moore's Judaism), we are very close indeed to the 6,000-year date in our history. Counting from the current year of 2010, we have 2010 + 4004 = 6014. The year of 6000 (or approximately so) is a specific line of demarcation in God's Plan as we shall see later. Thus, we shall take the date of Creation as Tishri 1(October 23), 4004 B.C.

Another observation we must make from Genesis 1:1 is contained in the Hebrew name translated in this verse as "God". The Hebrew word translated is Elohim. It is the most popular Hebrew name for God used in the Old Testament. As we mentioned in a previous chapter, the Bible is inspired in its original languages and not in its translated languages. Hebrew is quite different from English. It is a colorful, pictorial, and poetic language. Unlike

English, which is direct and logical, Hebrew oftentimes overlooks chronology and direct, logical perspective in order to emphasize and illustrate a story or message. In the original Hebrew, there are no vowels; thus, the placement of vowels and which vowels to incorporate are matters of pure speculation. Furthermore, in the original Hebrew there are many names for God, which are used in a substitutionary manner depending on which of God's many attributes are in view in any one place in the narrative. In English, there is only one name: God. Elohim is a particular Hebrew name for God which is a singular-plural noun. That the singular "God" is in view here cannot be doubted. However, the plural sense also suggests a plural "God". Many scholars have pored over this marvelous Hebrew name for God and concluded that the Christian doctrine of the Trinity is in view here: three separate persons in one Godhead. It seems that just as the English word for "man" can be taken as pertaining to a single man or all of mankind, the Hebrew word for God can refer to a singular Person in the Godhead or all three Persons. As we continue, we shall see other beautiful examples of slight variations in translation that reveal some very, amazing revelations. This is because God wants us to know Him and rewards our efforts when we try.

> It is the glory of God to conceal a thing: but the honour of kings is to search out a matter. (Prov 25:2)

The Hebrew word translated, as "created" is "bara". In its absolute sense and in reference to God, "bara" literally means "to create from nothing". This presents some interesting theological implications. Genesis 1:1 is saying that God, Elohim, created the heavens and the earth from nothing! Man cannot do this. If we were to mine some iron ore, smelt down the metal, reshape it, and forge it, we might "create" a hammer. In order to create this hammer however, we needed the raw materials beforehand. The sense of humanity's limited notion of "creation" implies that we merely gave the aspects and attributes of "hammer" to the raw material. This is true in every case of the sense of "creation" as applied to humanity. God, however, needed no raw materials; He did it from nothing.

> Through faith we understand that the worlds were framed by the word of God, so that things which are seen were not made of things which do appear. (Heb 11:3)

This is the very reason we capitalize the word "Creation" throughout this text. There is no comparable English word to the Hebrew word "bara". Is it any wonder why God chose the ancient Hebrew language to convey His Revelations to mankind?

The Gap Theory

In an obvious effort to satisfy the long ages required by historical geology and the theory of evolution, the Gap Theory was born. This theory implies that possibly billions of years elapsed between Genesis 1:1 and Genesis 1:2. To demonstrate this theory, we shall cite Genesis 1:2 and analyze it.

> And the earth was without form, and void; and darkness was upon the face of the deep. And the Spirit of God moved upon the face of the waters. (Gen 1:2)

Please take particular notice of the beginning phrase: "And the earth was without form, and void...". The Hebrew word translated as "without form" is "bohuw", and the Hebrew word translated as "void" is "tohuw". Some scholars argue that God's Creation, since He was perfect, would never have made the earth without form and void. Because of this, some catastrophe must have occurred between verses 1 and 2 to leave the earth in this condition. These scholars further propose that, sometime in the timeless past, Satan's rebellion took place on this earth (more on this in the next chapter). God, in His Judgment, brought a worldwide flood to earth to squash the rebellion. This flood, furthermore, accounts for the many fossilized dinosaur bones that can be supposedly dated back many millions of years ago. The earth, after this flood, was left without form and void. To make the earth habitable by man, God had to remake the earth.

Dr. Henry Morris and his colleagues at the Institute for Creation Research argue poignantly against this proposition. Since before Adam's fall death was unknown, dinosaur bones could not have been deposited before the fall of mankind. Furthermore, the Hebrew words "tohuw" and "bohuw" do not necessarily imply imperfection; they simply mean that God had other Creative work to do before He could make it habitable for mankind and life, in general. If the reader will carefully follow the rest of Genesis' Creation Week account, the land had to be separated from the waters, which covered the earth; the plants had to be created as food for the rest of Creation; the animals had to be Created; and, finally, man had to be Created. This is an interesting argument, indeed. We shall encounter more of the research performed by the scientists at the Institute for Creation Research further in our study.

Interestingly, many of the proponents of the original Gap Theory have since amended their story. They no longer adhere to the presence of dinosaurs contemporaneously with the rebellion of Satan. They have also changed their setting for Satan's rebellion. Some of the proponents of the Gap Theory now point to the asteroid belt between Mars and Jupiter as the locale for Satan's rebellion. They believe that the asteroids were, at one time, a planet which God destroyed because Satan's rebellion took place there. More of this theory can be obtained through the Internet.

The proponents of the old Gap Theory, however, continue to cling to their belief that Satan's original rebellion occurred on the earth and was thwarted by a worldwide flood. Some very influential, evangelical Christians, however, believe sincerely in this such as Jack Van Impe and the late C. I. Scofield.

Others, still holding to the original theory, point to these verses in Jeremiah:

> I beheld the earth, and, lo, it was without form, and void; and the heavens, and they had no light. I beheld the mountains, and, lo, they trembled, and all the hills moved lightly. I beheld, and, lo, there was no man,

> and all the birds of the heavens were fled. I beheld, and, lo, the fruitful place was a wilderness, and all the cities thereof were broken down at the presence of the LORD, and by his fierce anger. For thus hath the LORD said, The whole land shall be desolate; yet will I not make a full end. For this shall the earth mourn, and the heavens above be black: because I have spoken it, I have purposed it, and will not repent, neither will I turn back from it. (Jer 4:23-28)

Unless Jeremiah is retelling the story of the original Creation and then, immediately afterwards, the Flood, this passage would definitely support the original Gap Theory. After all, our hermeneutical basis would require its truthfulness since Scripture would then be supporting Scripture according to our rule 5. Notice however, the references to man and birds. These were only Created *after* the Gap Theory's story had taken place. Could God have Created mankind and the animal kingdom twice? This passage could also be a scriptural reference to the state of the earth after the Flood without any reference to the original Creation. Just because the earth was, once again, "without form and void" doesn't necessarily imply a reference to the Creation. I can't believe this to be the case because, according to the Plan I've propounded, Satan has yet to be judged, and I must still insist on Dr. Morris' explanation.

The Day/Age Theory

Again, in an apparent effort to satisfy so-called scientific criticism of great expanses of time required by evolutionists, some biblical scholars have proposed that the word translated as "day" from the Hebrew could refer to indefinitely long periods of time. We shall address this now.

> And God called the light Day, and the darkness he called Night. And the evening and the morning were the first day. (Gen 1:5)

Genesis 1:5 is the first time in the Bible the word "day" is used. Since the sun and moon were not Created until Genesis 1:16, the "light" and "darkness" supposedly had nothing to do with the literal 24-hour day that we experience now. Let us first analyze the words used for "light" and "darkness". In Genesis 1:3, God Creates "light". What this light is, we can't know since we're given no further explanations. But light is composed of a lot more than merely visible light; it is composed of electromagnetic waves. This is energy! God Created all the energy in the universe at this time as usable energy. In addition, the earth was obviously Created rotating on its axis. As it turned, one side of the earth faced this Created energy while the other side faced away.

This brings us to the definition of the Hebrew word translated as "day": "yom". Strong's Hebrew-Greek Concordance to the King James Version of the Bible defines "yom" thusly: from an unused root meaning to be hot; a day (as the warm hours), whether literal (from sunrise to sunset, or from one sunset to the next), or figurative (a space of time defined by an associated term), [often used adverb]. Please notice that the Hebrew word "yom" means either a 12-hour period signifying the daylight hours, a 24-hour period signifying the elapse of time between sunsets (this, by the way, is why the Jews measure their days as beginning at sunset), or an indefinite period of time further defined, in context, by an associated term. When used with a number, the Hebrew word, "yom", *always* means a 24-hour period. Notice that Genesis 1:5 calls this the *first* day. Thus, we are speaking here of a literal 24-hour period or one revolution of the earth on its axis. If God was trying to convey the idea of ages here, He would have used the Hebrew word "'olam" which means just that. We note the possibility that the earth, when it was first Created, probably had more energy and spin than it does today and the 24-hour period could be reduced to something like a 20-hour day. But we certainly cannot compromise with, nor give credence to, those critics who believe that each day was stretched out to incorporate vast elapses of time merely to satisfy some humanistic, scientific beliefs.

Age of the Universe

Evolutionary scientists have hypothesized that the universe is many billions of years old (something like 15 billion years). One claim they make is based on the speed of light. Some of the farthest stars in our universe are billions of light-years away. One light-year is the distance light travels at 186,000 miles per second in one year or 186,000 x 60 seconds x 60 minutes x 24 hours x 365 days = 5,865,696,000,000 miles! This is almost 6 trillion miles! Since these distant stars are billions of light-years away, it would require billions of years for their light to reach the earth; and since their light has reached the earth (or else we would never have seen them), the universe has to be billions of years old. This seems to be a strong argument with no apparent assumptions.

There is, however, one assumption that is inherent in this logic that is not easily uncovered: that the speed of light has remained constant since the birth of the universe. This has come under attack recently. We quote from the article entitled Speed of Light Slowing Down? by Chuck Missler in his newsletter, Personal Update, Volume 9, No. 1, January 1999:

> The Canadian mathematician, Alan Montgomery, has reported a computer analysis supporting the Setterfield/Norman results. His model indicates that the decay of the velocity of light closely follows a cosecant-squared curve, and has been asymptotic since 1958. If he is correct, the speed of light was 10-30% faster in the time of Christ; twice as fast in the days of Solomon; four times as fast in the days of Abraham, and perhaps more than 10 million times faster prior to 3000 B.C.

What an interesting development! If this hypothesis turns out to be true, its ramifications could be far-reaching. Both relativity and quantum mechanics would have to be revisited. It thoroughly explains the old age theories of the universe by exploding them and replacing them with a young age for the universe. To see why, let's calculate the time required for the light from the most distant star to reach earth under this new revelation. We would have $15*10^9/10^7 = 1500$ since 15 billion = $15*10^9$ and 10 million = 10^7. That is, it would require 1500 years for light from the farthest star to reach the earth at 10 million times the current speed of light. Since this new hypothesis only goes back to 3000 B.C., we still have another 1000 years to go backward to the Creation (4004 B.C.), and the speed of light would probably have been even faster. This time frame of 1500 years is easily within the time before the Flood.

Furthermore, astronomers believe that the most distant stars are speeding away from the center of the universe. How fast they're moving would definitely effect the calculation used to determine evolutionary estimates of the age of the universe. For example, how close were they 6,000 years ago? Have their velocities been constant? These and other considerations also effect the current age of the universe estimates.

Other dating methods, such as Carbon-14 dating, have recently been found to have flaws. Dating methods based on radioactive decay assume a certain amount of radioactive material to begin. Then, knowing how long it takes the radioactive substance to decay to half its original amount (called its half-life) and measuring the amount presently, it is a simple calculation to determine the age of the object the radioactive substance is contained in. This is the method used most often for fossil dating. All living things are carbon-based. Carbon has a normal atomic number of 12 (the number of protons or electrons). In the upper atmosphere, nitrogen, which has an atomic number of 14, is bombarded by incoming, cosmic radiation which strips some of its electrons off and changes it into the radioactive isotope called Carbon-14. Carbon-14 eventually makes its way to the surface of the earth and is ingested by plant life because plants need carbon dioxide for respiration and Carbon-14 and oxygen sometimes combine to form carbon dioxide. Animals, feeding on these plants or on each other, eventually ingest this Carbon-14. By assuming that fossils have originally the same amount of Carbon-14 in their tissue as comparably large plants and animals today, evolutionary scientists commit a grave error. They have assumed that the amount of Carbon-14 in our atmosphere today, and millions of years ago, has reached its equilibrium state: that the same amount of Carbon-14 is being created as is being destroyed. Experiments, however, have shown that for Carbon-14 to reach its equilibrium state requires 30,000 years! Furthermore, these experiments show that the equilibrium state will not be attained for another 20,000-25,000 years. This gives an approximate age to our atmosphere of 5,000-10,000 years – totally in accord with our hypothesis and Bishop Ussher's chronology.

Other evolutionary arguments sometimes allude to the "preposterous" notion that God, if He exists, would never have Created the earth with the "appearance" of age. But, why not? Were Adam and Eve Created as babies? No, they were Created as fully, functional adults. If they were, it follows that the plants and animals Created were also Created fully functional and mature. Otherwise, Adam and Eve may have had to wait a very long time before food was available to them, and they would have starved.

Living Conditions

At this point, we deem it appropriate to discuss the pre-flood, environmental living conditions for the existence of life. A lot of scientific research has gone into this aspect of the Bible especially by scientists at the Institute for Creation Research in San Diego, California. To begin this topic, we start at the verses in Genesis, which introduce it:

> And God said, Let there be a firmament in the midst of the waters, and let it divide the waters from the waters. And God made the firmament, and divided the waters which were under the firmament from the waters which were above the firmament: and it was so. And God called the firmament Heaven. And the evening and the morning were the second day. And God said, Let the waters under the heaven be gathered together unto one place, and let the dry land appear:

> and it was so. And God called the dry land Earth; and the gathering together of the waters called he Seas: and God saw that it was good. (Gen 1:6-10)

The Hebrew word translated as "firmament" is "raqiya" which literally means an expanse or open area. Therefore, if we read these verses carefully, we see that God originally Created the earth covered with water. Please notice that His first division of the waters divided the waters which were "under the firmament" from the waters which were above it. This is a vertical division! He did not divide the land from the sea until later. Creationist scientists understand, from this passage, that this means that water, in some form, was introduced into the pre-flood atmosphere. The most likely scientific scenario is that the water in the atmosphere was in the form of water vapor. This is the so-called **Water Vapor Canopy Theory**. What effects a water vapor canopy would have on life on the earth have been studied at some lengths. One book, The Waters Above by Joseph C. Dillow, is an excellently done scientific treatise on the effects of a 40-foot thick water vapor canopy on life on the earth. This would produce 2.18 atmospheres of pressure at sea level. Let the reader be forewarned, however, that this book is a highly technical treatise and only the technically inclined (i.e., those well-grounded in mathematics and physics) should attempt to read this book. Some of the effects discussed in the book include such topics as the increased air pressure on life, the increased lift that would allow such animals as pterodactyl (a flying reptile) to fly, the uniformly warm temperatures all across the globe, etc. For example, an aerodynamically moderate breeze of 16.4 mph would be required for a pterodactyl to gain lift in today's atmosphere. Only a gentle breeze of 11.6 mph would be required under the water vapor canopy. Some of the effects of a theoretical water vapor canopy are introduced in the Bible. One of these is the absence of rain:

> And every plant of the field before it was in the earth, and every herb of the field before it grew: for the LORD God had not caused it to rain upon the earth, and there was not a man to till the ground. But there

> **went up a mist from the earth, and watered the whole face of the ground. (Gen 2:5-6)**

Studies on a proposed water vapor canopy have concluded that the atmospheric turbulence that we experience today, and that produces rain, would be absent in the pre-flood atmosphere.

The water vapor canopy would separate the surface of the earth from the ozone layer higher above. It has been discovered that exposure to ozone has deleterious effects on life. In this way, the water vapor canopy could be partially responsible for the longevity of life as recorded in the pages of Genesis. To bring this point home, we quote from an article entitled The Pre-Flood Greenhouse Effect by Donald W. Patten in the volumes entitled A Symposium on Creation edited by Donald W. Patten:

> Prolonged ozone exposures of animals have caused (1) chronic pulmonary injury to lung tissue including bronchiolitis, and emphysematous and fibrotic changes in lung parenchyma, (2) agina, and (3) lung tumor acceleration. Ozone exposures of .1 to .2 ppm, 7 hours per day for 3 weeks caused an increase in mortality of newborn mice....
>
> Effects of Ozone on Animals. Ozone is a strong pulmonary irritant of the mucous membranes of animals. Even at very low concentrations such as are commonly found in community photochemical air pollution it augments the morbidity effects of respiratory infection and shortens the life span of test animals exposed to both respiratory infection and ozone. At high ozone levels as are found in certain occupational exposures, ozone causes acute lung injury in laboratory animals characterized by pulmonary congestion and edema; while at still higher concentrations, hemorrhage and death occur.
>
> Recent findings indicate that ozone may also produce secondary systemic effects on body metabolism and

> function. In addition, radiomimetic effects, where ozone simulates the effects of x-irradiation causing such effects as structural damage to myocardial tissue, increased rate in development of lung adenomas and *aging effects* have been reported particularly in prolonged exposures.

Please notice that exposure to ozone causes lung irritation, emphysema, bronchitis, damage to the heart (myocardial tissue), and lung cancer (adenomas). We have purposely highlighted the words "aging effects" (not italicized in the original) to drive our point home (as Donald Patten is trying to do). What is ozone? All animals need to breathe. Oxygen is the gas that is necessary for the breath of life. In nature, oxygen usually occurs in what is called a "diatomic" state, which merely means that normally two atoms of oxygen adhere together in a molecule. This is the form of oxygen that all animals need. Ozone is merely the adherence of three atoms of oxygen together (triatomically) in a molecule. Thus, respiration is normal and natural when we inhale oxygen diatomically but injurious and dangerous when we inhale it triatomically! I find it both interesting and remarkable that God, in His Providence, has Created man so delicately, and at the same time so endurably, that He can either protect us or punish us by simply causing slight imbalances in our environment.

Another positive effect that would be produced by a water vapor canopy is the increased air pressure. Here we quote from The Genesis Record by Henry M. Morris:

> Some have objected to the idea of a heavy vapor canopy because of the great increase in atmospheric pressure which it would cause at the earth's surface. Rather than being a problem, however, this effect would contribute still further to health and longevity. Modern biomedical research is increasingly proving that such "hyperbaric" pressures are very effective in combating disease and in promoting good health generally. There should be no problem in organisms living under

> high external pressures, provided their internal pressures had time to adjust correspondingly.

In fact, the beneficial effects resulting from high atmospheric pressures was discovered by chance when a diver, in a pressure chamber to prevent "bends", cut his hand, and it healed almost miraculously. Since then, people with arthritis, diabetes, and other chronic diseases have been helped greatly by hyperbaric pressure chambers such as those used by the National Hockey League to speed up the healing process to their injured athletes. In The Waters Above by Joseph C. Dillow, Dr. Dillow theorizes that the great bulk of the largest dinosaurs could *only* have been properly oxygenated by such high atmospheric pressures.

If the animals would have benefited by a water vapor canopy, what of plant life? It is readily apparent that plant life would have thrived in an atmosphere where there was high humidity, uniformly warm temperatures, rich soil, etc. As an example of a published report confirming the beneficial results of these conditions on plant life, we quote once again from Donald W. Patten's article entitled The Pre-Flood Greenhouse Effect in Volume 2 of A Symposium on Creation edited by Donald W. Patten:

> It may be of interest to the reader to note another type of artificial Greenhouse Effect under experimental research by the Kwick-Lok Industries of Yakima, Washington. Here barley seeds are experimentally laid out in pans in a type of large enclosed walk-in freezer type container. There are four small flourescent tubes, one in each corner. The trays of barley seed are kept under conditions of saturation and warm constant temperature. They are sprayed with water and nutrients six times daily. Under these conditions barley is seen to grow *9 to 11 inches high in 7 days, without sunlight and without soil.* This can theoretically be done in Alaska as easily as in California. This is an artificial Greenhouse Effect, bearing a few resemblances to

> the pre-flood world, where diurnal condensation and a permanent cloud cover prevailed.

To most readers, this is old news; it is the principles of "hydroponic gardening" which is practiced, today, around the world. Furthermore, many authors theorize further benefits to plant life due to the pre-flood atmosphere. For one thing, plants would grow more easily, grow larger, and provide greater nutritious value to the animals which fed off them (all animals, including man, were vegetarians. See Gen. 1:29-30). There could have been plants, before the Flood, that provided nutrients to the body for which we have no information today. For example, there could have been plants that provided a theoretical vitamin X for preventing diseases, both acute and chronic.

We have covered merely a sampling of some of the wonderful discoveries and theories that true, Creationist Scientists are uncovering today. Some more will be discussed at the end of the next chapter.

The Creation of Man

God Created man in His own "image". We shall attempt a discussion of this. For now, let us quote the Bible:

> And God said, Let us make man in our image, after our likeness: and let them have dominion over the fish of the sea, and over the fowl of the air, and over the cattle, and over all the earth, and over every creeping thing that creepeth upon the earth. So God created man in his own image, in the image of God created he him; male and female created he them. (Gen 1:26-27)

> And the LORD God formed man of the dust of the ground, and breathed into his nostrils the breath of life; and man became a living soul. (Gen 2:7)

> And the LORD God caused a deep sleep to fall upon Adam, and he slept: and he took one of his ribs,

> and closed up the flesh instead thereof; And the rib, which the LORD God had taken from man, made he a woman, and brought her unto the man. And Adam said, This is now bone of my bones, and flesh of my flesh: she shall be called Woman, because she was taken out of Man. Therefore shall a man leave his father and his mother, and shall cleave unto his wife: and they shall be one flesh. And they were both naked, the man and his wife, and were not ashamed. (Gen 2:21-25)

The very first thing we must address here is why there are two versions of Creation in the Bible: Genesis Chapter 1 and Genesis Chapter 2. This is a curious reflection of the ancient language of Hebrew that was already alluded to. Stories were not told chronologically. Sometimes, and in this case, generalities were touched upon and then, later, more specific details were discussed.

In the Creation story, God Created the man and the woman in His own "image". The Hebrew word used for "image" is the same one used to describe idols, shadows, etc. Thus, Hebrew sheds no new light on what this "image" is. Obviously, the word "image" does not necessarily mean that we look like God. Most theologians agree that this word means that we have many of God's attributes but in a finite rather than an infinite capacity. In fact:

> God is a Spirit: and they that worship him must worship him in spirit and in truth. (John 4:24)

> No man hath seen God at any time; the only begotten Son, which is in the bosom of the Father, he hath declared him. (John 1:18)

> No man hath seen God at any time. If we love one another, God dwelleth in us, and his love is perfected in us. (I Jn 4:12)

The Bible emphasizes, in many places, that, because God is a Spirit, He has never been seen. God, unlike us, has no body. When Moses wished to see God, God commanded him to hide himself and look only upon His back as He passed because to look upon God would cause Moses' death.

> **And he said, Thou canst not see my face: for there shall no man see me, and live. And the LORD said, Behold, there is a place by me, and thou shalt stand upon a rock: And it shall come to pass, while my glory passeth by, that I will put thee in a clift of the rock, and will cover thee with my hand while I pass by: And I will take away mine hand, and thou shalt see my back parts: but my face shall not be seen. (Exod 33:20-23)**

Thus, this "image" cannot be taken as literally as it appears. Our "spirits", however, may be the "image" of God. We, like God, have the attributes of love, justice, reasoning, morality, etc. These we have, unlike God, in a limited capacity. One caution that we must make here concerns the Incarnation of Jesus where He continually said that anyone who has seen Him has seen God. He was obviously not referring to Himself physically but rather spiritually otherwise the Bible would contradict itself. The body that is inhabited by Jesus is to allow mankind to communicate directly with God.

Another thing that must be mentioned here concerns the institution of marriage. Because the woman was taken from man, for either one to be complete they must be united in marriage. This is the only way God recognizes the proper means for intercourse and conception. Furthermore, the only time that a married couple is complete is when they unite in sexual intercourse because men and women, in many ways, have exactly opposite characteristics of each other. The institution of marriage was done for all regardless of class, race, beliefs, religion, etc. Please notice that this marriage was not conducted in a Church, Synagogue, Government Office, etc.; it was consummated when the two joined in sexual intercourse. Thus, sexual intercourse (whether performed in the classical way or otherwise) binds the sexual partners in marriage.

> Know ye not that your bodies are the members of Christ? shall I then take the members of Christ, and make them the members of an harlot? God forbid. What? know ye not that he which is joined to an harlot is one body? for two, saith he, shall be one flesh. But he that is joined unto the Lord is one spirit. Flee fornication. Every sin that a man doeth is without the body; but he that committeth fornication sinneth against his own body. What? know ye not that your body is the temple of the Holy Ghost which is in you, which ye have of God, and ye are not your own? For ye are bought with a price: therefore glorify God in your body, and in your spirit, which are God's. (1 Cor 6:15-20)

Paul is saying this in conjunction with one of the pagan practices of the city of Corinth. It was a pagan, customary practice in Corinth that men could go to a pagan temple where harlots were available. Furthermore, these harlots were available for the men to have intercourse with in conjunction with their beliefs of the gods. In other words, it was not merely alright for men to engage in this behavior; it was expected! Paul is admonishing this pagan custom as abominable in the sight of God because, as he argues, that men who practice this are "joining" their bodies, in marriage, to harlots! In order to seal this point, it's only necessary to quote Jesus.

> It hath been said, Whosoever shall put away his wife, let him give her a writing of divorcement: But I say unto you, That whosoever shall put away his wife, saving for the cause of fornication, causeth her to commit adultery: and whosoever shall marry her that is divorced committeth adultery. (Matt 5:31-32)

God obviously intended the union of marriage, and family, to teach the concepts of love and obedience to family members. Children are to obey and love their parents; parents are to love and discipline their children. Likewise, the man and woman are to be united in a loving, and spiritual, way in order to give an orderly direction for the entire family. This is the kind of love God expects from us. We are to love and obey God as a child does his natural parents realizing that, as our Father, He loves us and disciplines us for our own good.

The Fall of Man Revisited

God gave one restriction to the man: not to eat of the fruit of the Tree of Knowledge of Good and Evil.

> **And the LORD God commanded the man, saying, Of every tree of the garden thou mayest freely eat: But of the tree of the knowledge of good and evil, thou shalt not eat of it: for in the day that thou eatest thereof thou shalt surely die. (Gen 2:16-17)**

Please notice that God commanded the *man*. Eve, the woman, had not yet been Created. God often does this. He works through the agency of man; the man was obviously expected to pass this information to the woman. As we shall see, he did.

God's command was not merely meant to test the man, Adam, and the woman, for God wished that Adam and Eve would trust Him to protect them from evil. If they did not know that good and evil existed, they were innocent; everything that they said, thought, or did was good by definition.

God, however, allowed Adam and Eve to be tempted. He wished that they would continue to innocently trust Him for all their needs. They didn't! The serpent was entered into by Satan (there are many references in the Bible that state this) and tempted Eve to eat of the fruit. She, in turn, offered the fruit to Adam who also ate of it. Thus, they both disobeyed God.

> Now the serpent was more subtil than any beast of the field which the LORD God had made. And he said unto the woman, Yea, hath God said, Ye shall not eat of every tree of the garden? And the woman said unto the serpent, We may eat of the fruit of the trees of the garden: But of the fruit of the tree which is in the midst of the garden, God hath said, Ye shall not eat of it, neither shall ye touch it, lest ye die. And the serpent said unto the woman, Ye shall not surely die: For God doth know that in the day ye eat thereof, then your eyes shall be opened, and ye shall be as gods, knowing good and evil. And when the woman saw that the tree was good for food, and that it was pleasant to the eyes, and a tree to be desired to make one wise, she took of the fruit thereof, and did eat, and gave also unto her husband with her; and he did eat. And the eyes of them both were opened, and they knew that they were naked; and they sewed fig leaves together, and made themselves aprons. (Gen 3:1-7)

The story of the events of the Fall can be very instructive. Firstly, the serpent obviously allowed Satan to enter him. Otherwise, God's later Judgment on the serpent would make no sense. Secondly, there is no mention that the man was ever directly tempted; the woman was approached because Satan knew that the man would never give in.

> And Adam was not deceived, but the woman being deceived was in the transgression. (1 Tim. 2:14)

Thirdly, Satan carefully mixed the truth with enough half-truths and lies to make his plea sound appealing. Fourthly, the woman misquoted God when she said, "neither shall ye touch it...". Either she had her own perception of God's express command (i.e., she may have thought that it was an unfair restriction), or Adam may not have communicated God's command to her correctly. Fifthly, Adam did not question the woman; he simply partook of the fruit. Lastly, the Bible says that their eyes were opened; they knew they were naked, and they sewed fig leaves together to cover their nakedness.

Let's analyze this a little further. Was Satan lying? After all, weren't their eyes opened to know the difference between good and evil? The answer is yes! When Satan said, "Ye shall not surely die.", he knew that they would. Satan knew God's Justice, and that He meant what He said - "for in the day that thou eatest thereof thou shalt surely die." Notice that God said that they would surely die in the *day* that they ate the fruit. The Hebrew word used is "yowm" which is similar in meaning to "yom" and should be translated as "day".

Did they die the day they partook of the fruit? According to most theologians, they died spiritually - that is, they were separated from God. While this is true, it is not a completely satisfactory answer. Let us quote from the Bible.

> And all the days that Adam lived were nine hundred and thirty years: and he died. (Gen 5:5)

> But, beloved, be not ignorant of this one thing, that one day is with the Lord as a thousand years, and a thousand years as one day. (2 Pet 3:8)

Notice that Adam did not live a thousand years, which is a *day* with the Lord. This, then, is a wonderful confirmation of the Dispensational Theory!

Furthermore, Satan knew when they partook of the fruit they would lose their innocence and, hence, their protection from God. Because of his (i.e., Satan's) power and intellect compared to the man and woman and God's withdrawal of His protection, Satan could now easily usurp man's dominion over the earth.

The Age of Innocence ended with God's curse.

> And the LORD God said unto the serpent, Because thou hast done this, thou art cursed above all cattle, and above every beast of the field; upon thy belly shalt

> thou go, and dust shalt thou eat all the days of thy life: And I will put enmity between thee and the woman, and between thy seed and her seed; it shall bruise thy head, and thou shalt bruise his heel. Unto the woman he said, I will greatly multiply thy sorrow and thy conception; in sorrow thou shalt bring forth children; and thy desire shall be to thy husband, and he shall rule over thee. And unto Adam he said, Because thou hast hearkened unto the voice of thy wife, and hast eaten of the tree, of which I commanded thee, saying, Thou shalt not eat of it: cursed is the ground for thy sake; in sorrow shalt thou eat of it all the days of thy life; Thorns also and thistles shall it bring forth to thee; and thou shalt eat the herb of the field; In the sweat of thy face shalt thou eat bread, till thou return unto the ground; for out of it wast thou taken: for dust thou art, and unto dust shalt thou return. (Gen 3:14-19)

The Fall of Man was a sin which aberrated everything. The woman would now be subservient to her husband and have pain in childbirth. The ground, which before so easily yielded its production, would now become resistant to grow edible food. Death was introduced into the world; Adam's sin nature, and death, would be passed onto his seed from henceforth ("for dust thou art, and unto dust shalt thou return.")

For another thing, the man and woman were barred from the Garden of Eden because the Tree of Life was there. Obviously, access to the Tree of Life would allow Adam and Eve to continue to live on indefinitely. God did not want this. Why? Well for one thing, He promised the man that the day he ate of the fruit of the Tree of Knowledge of Good and Evil he would die; allowing access to the Tree of Life would nullify God's punishment. But there is a more subtle and beautiful reason why God did this. Man was now imperfect and irreconcilable to a perfect God. But God, because of His infinite capacity to love, wanted to spend eternity with man. In order to spend eternity with mankind, man must shed his corrupted and irreconcilable body. God's Justice and Love would both be satisfied to do this. This is one reason why He instituted His Plan from the beginning.

Chapter 5

DISPENSATION 2: CONSCIENCE

As we have seen, there is a great deal to the Bible, and truth in general, that is not readily apparent. In fact, we're going to visit some aspects of Scripture in this Dispensation that embodies the statement "Truth is stranger than fiction". We exclaim, with the circus barker, "You ain't seen nothin' yet." This Age is covered by Genesis Chapters 4 through 8.

After the Age of Innocence, God Dispensed a new means for Judging mankind: conscience. This was manifested to Cain when he killed his brother, Abel. Cain and Abel were Adam's and Eve's sons. Whether they were Adam's only sons at the time, we can't know since the Bible is silent about this. Ancient Jewish scholars, however, believe, according to tradition, that Adam and Eve had over one hundred children. Cain and Abel were to provide offerings to the Lord. Abel sacrificed a sheep, and Cain made a vegetable offering. God told Cain that He was displeased with Cain's offering and attempted to encourage him to do better next time since He knew that Cain became very discouraged with God's displeasure. In order to know what kinds of sacrifices God demanded, He obviously had to communicate this previously even though this is not recorded. Doctor Henry Morris of the ICR makes the logical argument that God had already commanded to mankind what actions of men were pleasing and sinful to God even before the official act of giving the Ten Commandments. What Cain couldn't (or wouldn't) understand was that God demanded blood sacrifices to satisfy His Justice. These sacrifices were merely substitutes to point men to the future, perfect sacrifice of Jesus. But jealousy swelled in Cain's heart against his brother, Abel. Man now had a sin nature because he now knew about good and evil. Cain eventually murdered his own brother, Abel. For punishment, God sent Cain away from Adam's family.

There are two questions that are not directly answered by the Bible that people continually bring up: Cain's wife and Cain's mark. We shall deal with these together. Cain, in a fit of fear, remarked to God that once he was sent from Adam's, and thus God's, presence, he would be slain by others. God placed a mark on Cain warning mankind that whosoever slew Cain would suffer a sevenfold judgment at the hands of God. What this mark was the Bible does not say, but it must've been a visible mark. This whole story can be found in Genesis Chapter 4. Who were these other people? Would Cain have married a woman from these other people? Let us first notice the longevity of the people living at this time: over 900 years. That this is literally their ages is without question since they were capable of having children at the same ages we do today. How many children could a couple have in 900 years? Quite a few! Not only that, but their genes were perfect. There was no *genetic load* (i.e., no mutations to pass onto their offspring). Over time, the genetic load builds in the human race and allows for the greater possibility of mutations. Since there was no genetic load at this time, God had not yet issued His command to refrain from incest. Furthermore, the Bible states that Adam and Eve had other children (see Genesis 5:4). Thus, these other people were the offspring of Adam and Eve, and Cain's wife was either one of Adam's daughters or an offspring of one of Adam's children. Could anyone, in fairness, believe that all of Adam's sons and daughters remained at home?

We hope we have addressed these two so-called "unanswerable questions" of unbelievers sufficiently. Because we have neither the time nor space to give a more detailed analysis, we must move on. For those wishing a more thorough discussion, we recommend The Genesis Record by Henry M. Morris. At this time, we turn our attention to some of the more salient points of this Dispensation.

Sin

Many theologians, down through the centuries, have puzzled over this aspect of man. What is sin? The very first sin involved disobedience to God and resulted in man's Fall. We have already addressed the question of which of Adam's or Eve's sin was greater: Adam's because he openly defied and rejected God. If Adam would not have partaken of the forbidden fruit, would Eve still have been punished? We believe so because God always means what He says. We don't know, however, how the punishment would have differed. Perhaps He would have separated Eve from Adam and Created another female companion for Adam. Regardless, we do know that Adam rejected God for Eve. This was an act of rebellion against God. Once they both ate of the fruit and their eyes were opened, it seems that rebellion became part of their natures. However the fruit that affected them was obviously passed onto their offspring throughout the ages. It was passed physically. This means that their bodies were affected. Quite often our bodies desire, or need, to have something that our minds (i.e., our consciences) know is wrong. It could be drugs which we know, if we become addicted, will eventually destroy us. It could be illicit sex which we realize that we could partake of and not harm us physically. Either way, it will harm our consciences. Once we have allowed ourselves to disobey our consciences, the sin becomes easier, and more severe, the next time.

At this point, we must recognize the construction of man. I believe that man is a tripartite being. This simply means that man is composed of three parts: body, soul, and spirit. The Bible mentions these three parts of man's being throughout its pages. Since some passages in the Bible use the terms "soul" and "spirit" interchangeably, some theologians believe that man is really composed of two parts. We shall not attempt to answer this charge except to refer the reader to the booklet The Doctrine of Man by Harold L. Willmington. J. R. Church, in an article entitled Home of the Soul in his wonderfully done prophetic magazine Prophecy in the News dated February, 1999, does an excellent job in separating the soul from the spirit. Anyway, suffice it to say that we all know that our bodies are the seat of the senses where we interact with our environment. Our souls are the seat of our emotions; our spirits are the seat of our intellect. Somehow, our soul and spirit are intertwined; our bodies are separate. We shall address this shortly. How does our soul and spirit control our bodies? A modern neurosurgeon, named Wilder Penfield, was performing experiments on the brain to map out where specific functions were controlled. Each time he provided a slight, electrical charge to the part of the brain known as the Sylvan fissure, his patient would invariably say something to the effect that he was now leaving his body! This makes sense. There must be some physical point of our body that the spirit and soul must interact with the body. Thus, the question of life after death is convincingly answered. Interestingly if this point exists, does it not make sense that Satan and his minions also know where this point is? This, then, would be the point at which demonic possession (which I do believe exists) occurs. This is why God commands us to never lose control of our mental faculties. Drunkenness, drugs, and certain far Eastern techniques to "empty" one's mind allow evil spirits to gain control over us.

If the soul and spirit can survive without the body and God knows this, the simple solution would be for God to replace our bodies since they are the part of us that has been corrupted. This He does with the Christian, Jewish, and Islamic doctrine of **resurrection**. Please understand that no other religions in the world believe this doctrine thus making Christianity, Judaism, and Islam unique. But God will not allow our original bodies to completely perish since He originally made them in perfection. Somehow He knows where the specific part of our body is after death so that He can restore and remake our bodies in a grander, more spiritual style. When our bodies are destroyed through cremation, simple decay, etc. the matter that composes our bodies is not lost; it is simply transformed into another state. If there is a single molecule that God can keep track of to restore our bodies, He does. He may even have our DNA structure recorded so that He can easily reconstruct our bodies with minor changes. This is the so-called **Germ Theory**. There are other theories which can be read about in any standard theology text. Whatever theory we adopt, it is necessary that we believe what God says: that *this* body is the one that will one day be resurrected.

Please notice that Satan is nowhere mentioned in the sin of Cain. Whether we are to conclude from this that Satan did not tempt Cain we cannot say. Where God is silent about a matter, we should be also. For another thing, please notice the progression of sins that have occurred to this point. First, Eve disobeys God. Next, Adam rebels against God. Finally, Cain strikes down his brother. The patriarchs (i.e., the first people) progressed from simple disobedience to God to murder! The severest sins that we obviously commit are against God because, once we rationalize these, it is a simple progression to rationalize sin against each other. If we could somehow avoid committing sins against God, perhaps we could avoid sins against our fellow man. We have already addressed God's provisions for the forgiveness of our sins. More importantly, we must ask God to forgive us for our sin nature: our natural propensity to sin. Our willfulness (i.e., our rebelliousness), however, prevents us from coming to God in the first place. But God's Plan is not only Perfect, it is Complete. When we get to Dispensation VI: Grace, we will discover that God's Plan also incorporates a way for us to sin no longer.

Rebellion of the World

Soon after men began to multiply on the face of the Earth, they began to rebel against God. Dr. Morris has calculated some interesting population statistics for the antediluvian (i.e., pre-flood) world. He shows, both in his The Genesis Record and The Biblical Basis for Modern Science, that the antediluvian world, with birth and death rates both accounted for, possibly had a population in the billions just before the Flood. Furthermore with man's longevity, his more perfect intellect, his more perfect physique, etc. than man possesses today, his sins would be multiplied manifold, in both severity and number, over the sins that we commit today.

The first mention, in the Bible, of mankind's general rebellion is:

> And to Seth, to him also there was born a son; and he called his name Enos: then began men to call upon the name of the LORD. (Gen 4:26)

Admittedly, this verse sounds as though men were turning towards God. We have already addressed this verse as the first biblical mention of outward blasphemy in the antediluvian (i.e., pre-Flood) world because (remember?) it should be translated as men "profaning the name of God".

How was this outward rebellion so wicked and perverse that the Bible specifically names it? We now address this from an interesting perspective:

> And it came to pass, when men began to multiply on the face of the earth, and daughters were born unto them, That the sons of God saw the daughters of men that they were fair; and they took them wives of all which they chose. And the LORD said, My spirit shall not always strive with man, for that he also is flesh: yet his days shall be an hundred and twenty years. There were giants in the earth in those days; and also after that, when the sons of God came in unto the daughters of men, and they bare children to them, the same became mighty men which were of old, men of renown. And GOD saw that the wickedness of man was great in the earth, and that every imagination of the thoughts of his heart was only evil continually. (Gen 6:1-5)

A very mysterious passage, indeed! Firstly, this passage refers to beings known as the "sons of God". Who are they? The Hebrew for "sons of God" is "bene Elohiym". These Hebrew words, when used together, are *always*, throughout the Bible, used for angels. Thus, the "sons of God" are angels. The phrase "daughters of men" is "bath 'adam" in the Hebrew. Adam, the name of the first man, literally means "man", or "earth", in the Hebrew. Thus, these "daughters of men" were literally human women. The phrase "they took them wives of all which they chose." connotes that angels selected human women to copulate with. What was the angels' purpose? Further on down the passage says of the women that "they bare children to them". These men became "mighty men which were of old, men of renown." This, in the original Hebrew, is a *negative* reference. Just as we, today, have our heroes to whom we accord great respect, we also have villains that we all know about. The heroes are famous; the villains are *infamous*. Even though we may accord a great deal of respect to both groups, we neither love nor admire the villains. This is what the Bible is trying to say. These offspring are called "Nephilim" in the original Hebrew. This word literally means "the fallen ones". To men, it means "bullies" or "tyrants". Please notice their physical stature: "There were giants in the earth in those days". Some have objected to this translation saying that the Hebrew connotes more in the way of evil people, but the seventy Jewish translators of the Septuagint (i.e., the translation into Greek) translated this word into the Greek "gigantes" which literally means giants. Furthermore, Josephus, in his Antiquities of the Jews, states that these people were, indeed, giants. It is only a more modern approach, popularized by Augustine that has suggested that the "sons of God" were from the godly line of Seth and that the "daughters of men" were of the ungodly line of Cain thus producing evil offspring. This argument fails on several accounts. We have already shown that Enos, of Seth's supposed godly line, was the first to openly rebel against God. For a more complete argument as to who the Nephilim were and an argument against the so-called Seth lineage theory, see the book Alien Encounters by Chuck Missler and Mark Eastman. For more research on giants in the earth's past, I also highly recommend Genesis 6 Giants by Stephen Quayle.

So, then, why did the "angels of god" produce these offspring? We believe, with the ancient Jews, that these were *fallen* angels! These were the angels who sided with Lucifer against God. They obviously did this to corrupt the race of mankind that God originally Created. If we hearken back to the Protevangelium (Gen. 3:15), Satan understood that the "seed of the woman" had to be an uncorrupted man. If Satan bred only these corrupted Nephilim who were not human, the "seed of the woman" could never be born (i.e., Jesus)! What's more, Chuck Missler hypothesizes that, since demons are disembodied spirits, the Nephilim that have since perished are today without bodies, unlike us or the angels, and are today's demons. Stephen Quayle's second book, Aliens & Fallen Angels, is excellently done, well researched, and a must read for the serious Christian who is curious about how Satan will once again use Nephilim for the last days.

Many have objected to the notion of a loving God because of many of God's Judgments on humanity in the Old Testament. They say that a kind, loving, and merciful God could never visit such horrific acts on humanity if He loves mankind. I, too, was once caught in this mode of thought, but I decided that God, in His own time, would reveal the answer to me. This was it! Please notice that only Noah's generations were uncorrupted by this angelic intrusion. Thus, Shem, Ham, and Japheth, from Noah's line and their wives, were also uncorrupted. This makes Noah's line the only *true* human beings left on earth. Therefore, the only beings who were Judged by the ensuing Flood were not really human or were wicked beyond belief. Furthermore, the Bible does not say that Shem, Ham, Japheth, or their wives were righteous. This fact should further our argument that God wished merely to Judge the offspring of the corrupted race and those who gave themselves to them and not just to save the righteous. As we read on in the Bible, we encounter further Judgments of God on whole tribes in which the Hebrews were instructed to annihilate every living creature: men, women, children, and their beasts. A careful reading of the Scriptures indicates that these, too, were Nephilim. But why beasts, you might ask? Does anyone think, for a moment, that Satan is above ordering his minions to engage in bestiality?

In fact when one considers the gigantic proportions of some of the dinosaurs, it is easy to conjecture that these may have been the result of angelic sexual intrusion.

The Flood

God could not have the race of man corrupted with Satan's seed and send His Messiah because only man, according to God's own promise, could rule the Earth. The Messiah must be a man. This was a great dilemma for God. Judgment surely had to come upon the antediluvian world.

> And GOD saw that the wickedness of man was great in the earth, and that every imagination of the thoughts of his heart was only evil continually. And it repented the LORD that he had made man on the earth, and it grieved him at his heart. (Gen 6:5-6)

The next verse tells us what God had committed to do.

> And the LORD said, I will destroy man whom I have created from the face of the earth; both man, and beast, and the creeping thing, and the fowls of the air; for it repenteth me that I have made them. (Gen 6:7)

God had, by now, resigned Himself to destroy all flesh from the Earth. Why all flesh? Obviously because the animals had also become corrupted. Remember, it was a serpent in the Garden of Evil that allowed Satan to enter it. But could God still salvage His original Plan of Redemption for mankind?

> But Noah found grace in the eyes of the LORD. These are the generations of Noah: Noah was a just man and perfect in his generations, and Noah walked with God. (Gen 6:8-9)

God found one family in the antediluvian world that was uncorrupted - Noah and his family. We have thrown in the quotation for verse 9 to emphasize the point that Noah was not merely a "just man" (i.e., a saved man). The phrase "perfect in his generations", according to Chuck Missler, quite plausibly means that Noah's genealogy was uncorrupted by the evil unions that had already corrupted the rest of the antediluvian world. Why else would there be two mysterious references to Noah's godliness (viz., "a just man" and "perfect in his generations") in this single passage? This, then, must mean that God had found a whole family of mankind with which He could salvage His Plan!

But how was God going to destroy all flesh and, at the same time, spare Noah's family to repopulate the Earth? He would instruct Noah to build a boat and then send a worldwide flood!

> And, behold, I, even I, do bring a flood of waters upon the earth, to destroy all flesh, wherein is the breath of life, from under heaven; and every thing that is in the earth shall die. (Gen 6:17)

Such a prediction of a universal flood backed by a lot of rain must've had an unbelieving aspect to the rest of the world. Before the Flood, mankind had never experienced rain.

> And every plant of the field before it was in the earth, and every herb of the field before it grew: for the LORD God had not caused it to rain upon the earth, and there was not a man to till the ground. But there went up a mist from the earth, and watered the whole face of the ground. (Gen 2:5-6)

Imagine, if you will, some preacher making these dire predictions of rain causing a worldwide flood destroying all life when mankind had never experienced rain. Most, if not all, would consider such a preacher as a crazy man. Perhaps this was God's intention.

Then in order to save His originally Created life, God would send two of every kind of animal to Noah to place on the "ark" and to repopulate the Earth after the Flood. Immediately, questions arise. Is it possible for at least two of every kind of animal to fit on Noah's boat? This obviously must include the mammoth dinosaurs besides gigantic mammals such as elephants. Dr. Henry Morris has calculated that the average size for all the possible *fully grown* animals that would have to enter the ark was approximately the size of one of today's sheep. Please remember that the biblical narrative nowhere addresses that the animals entering the ark were *fully grown*. The dimensions of the ark were 300 cubits x 50 cubits x 30 cubits. A cubit has been estimated to be about 1½ feet. Thus, the modern dimensions were 450 feet x 75 feet x 45 feet. This is a gigantic boat! Only some of the modern, luxury liners have dimensions greater than this. What about carnivores occupying cramped quarters with herbivores that were normally their prey? Again, we emphasize that all animals, including man, were vegetarians before the Flood. How about the food that must be stored and the resulting excrement that had to be continually cleaned? If God could somehow *call* the animals to board the ark, He could also bring a deep sleep (i.e., hibernation) to fall upon them.

What of the Flood itself? What, for example, repercussions would befall the planet as the result of a worldwide flood? For one thing, mountains and valleys would be instantly created. Many of the animals, and probably men, would be instantly caught in the currents and eddies created and be deposited in sediment where fossilization could instantly occur. The recent eruption of Mt. St. Helens demonstrates the probability of the immediacy of the creation of gigantic rifts and valleys (such as the Grand Canyon) and fossilization. The soil, once perfect and unmixed, would now be mixed with garbage soil from all layers thereby creating less favorable conditions for farming. The water vapor canopy would be condensed out thusly eliminating it with its wonderful protective powers and worldwide greenhouse effect. The atmosphere would become turbulent and allow mankind to become subject to all kinds of weather calamities. Mankind, with all this protection removed, would no longer be able to enjoy the fruits of longevity. The heavens would now become visible, which they weren't (i.e., completely) while the water vapor canopy was in place (the canopy would have allowed a "hazy" view of the heavens), and men could now see the stars clearly. More on this will be covered in the next chapter. The Flood took place, according to the chronology that we've already established, some time about 4,500 years ago, or 2500 B.C. But, someone might object, the biblical record gives several generations of people from the Creation to the Flood. If it is remembered that the long lifetimes of the patriarchs approach 1,000 years and their child-bearing years begin at about age 100, there is no problem with this. I invite the reader to count the years of each patriarch's age to the time of the Flood, and I'm confident that the reader will come up with approximately the same chronology. The most important thing, from our revelational viewpoint, is that the Flood was God's way of summarily ending the Dispensation of Conscience.

Scientific confirmation for the Flood abounds in many works. Besides Velikovsky's book, Earth in Upheaval, books such as The Genesis Flood by Morris and Whitcomb and The Waters Above by Joseph C. Dillow contain interesting arguments for the reality of the occurrence of a worldwide flood. The book, The Genesis Flood, is a geological perspective of the world as it exists today. Many questions are raised that no uniformitarian (i.e., evolutionist) can satisfactorily address but that can easily be explained in terms of a global deluge. As an example, let's address the existence of marine fossils discovered at the tops of mountain peaks. The naturalistic explanation maintains that these mountains were raised from the ocean floor! The biblical explanation is much simpler: the waters actually covered all the mountain peaks. Or let's address polystrate fossils. Polystrate fossils are fossils that actually traverse several geological ages based on the rock strata they're contained in since, according to evolutionary geologists, differing rock strata represent different evolutionary ages. But how can this be? Surely these fossils would have rotted during the millions of years required to lay down the different strata. But they didn't! Is it possible that these strata were actually laid down in rushing flood waters over a very short duration of time?

In Joseph C. Dillow's work, The Waters Above, the author makes meticulous scrutiny over the text of Scripture and analyzes what Moses meant in his record of Genesis. The ancient Hebrew is rigorously scrutinized for its meaning, grammar, and context. Then,

Dr. Dillow alludes to other cultural references to a worldwide flood. Finally, he creates a scientific model replete with ten predictions of the ramifications of a 40 foot water vapor canopy enveloping the earth. He then goes on to provide scientific analyses of the probability of these predictions.

Since Drs. Morris, Whitcomb, and Dillow are all professing Christians, Dr. Velikovsky's work takes on more importance. He is obviously not a professing Christian based on many of his remarks in his book. For example, he makes light of Bishop Ussher's date of 4004 B.C. for the year of Creation and then makes the farther remark that he (Dr. Velikovsky) cannot understand why a young earth favors creationism over evolution! He even proposes a newer, more consistent, theory of evolution! The important thing to consider here is that Dr. Velikovsky, a non-Christian naturalist, argues for the occurrence of a worldwide Flood and the reality of a young earth.

As an interesting aside, let's address Noah's drunkenness after the Flood. Any search through the Scriptures will reveal that God, even though throughout the Bible condemns drunkenness, never condemns Noah's intoxication. Why? Dr. Henry Morris in his The Genesis Record cites an interesting reason. Before the Flood with its increased atmospheric pressure, would cause the chemical reaction producing fermentation in the grapes to proceed much more slowly than after the Flood. He even goes so far as to suggest the chemical equation involved. Thus, Noah was actually caught off guard and drank wine that was much more potent than he was accustomed to!

Adam and Eve Revisited

An interesting discovery was just made by geneticists. I'll repeat Chuck Missler's Personal Update for September 2006, Volume 16, No. 9 under the heading "Written for a Generation to Come"

> Genetic anthropology is conducted using the Y-chromosome and mitochondrial DNA, two segments that have unique properties that

facilitate studies of multigenerational inheritance. Y-chromosome DNA is passed only from father to son; similarly, mitochondrial DNA is passed only from the mother to her offspring. In addition, both accumulate changes at a predictable rate, producing genetic "bread crumbs" that make it possible to follow these bread crumbs (markers) as a population moved around the globe.

Intriguingly, in light of current scientific knowledge, the Bible seems to mention DNA itself: "Thine eyes did see my substance, yet being unperfect; and in thy book all my members were written, which in continuance were fashioned, when as yet there was none of them" (Psalm 139:16), as well as its recent potential to record both the time and the places where people lived: God "has made of one blood every nation of men to dwell upon the whole face of the earth, having determined ordained times and the boundaries of their dwelling" (Acts 17:26).

The field of genetic anthropology, which allowed man's history to be studied with DNA, first gained public awareness in 1987 with the announcement that mitochondrial DNA analysis had demonstrated that every human being on the planet descended from the same female. Similar analysis of Y-chromosomes found that every human male was also descended from a single individual human male. Scientists involved (gleefully) proclaimed that, since this identified male lived considerably after the female, the Bible had been officially repudiated, with headlines across the globe declaring "Adam and Eve Never Met!"

The scientists may need to review their Sunday School lessons. What "mitochondrial Eve" and "Y-chromosome Adam" really represent are really statistical entities called the Most Recent Common

> Ancestor, or MRCA, meaning the last shared relative. As such, they exquisitely confirm the biblical account. Since the males on the ark were Noah and his sons, all should have had identical Y-chromosomes. The four women, however (Mrs. Noah, Ham, Shem, and Japheth), ostensibly not related, would therefore trace their maternal lineages back to the Biblical Eve. The MRCA of the men, then, was Noah, but the MRCA of the maternal lineage was NOT Mrs. Noah, but Eve – who did (according to both science and the Bible) live considerably before her statistical counterpart, Noah.

Once again, the biblical narrative is validated. What would be even more intriguing would be what genetic anthropologists would find if they were able to trace back the number of *generations* to the MRCAs. They would undoubtedly find that these generations would include thousands, not millions, of years!

Chapter 6

DISPENSATION 3: GOVERNMENT

We shall not spend any time on the duration that the Flood waters covered the Earth. This is a lengthy topic for another treatise. The next age, the Age of Government, is covered by Genesis Chapters 9 through 11. We shall now demonstrate that God initiated this new dispensation, or age, with a command to Noah.

> And God blessed Noah and his sons, and said unto them, Be fruitful, and multiply, and replenish the earth. And the fear of you and the dread of you shall be upon every beast of the earth, and upon every fowl of the air, upon all that moveth upon the earth, and upon all the fishes of the sea; into your hand are they delivered. Every moving thing that liveth shall be meat for you; even as the green herb have I given you all things. But flesh with the life thereof, which is the blood thereof, shall ye not eat. And surely your blood of your lives will I require; at the hand of every beast will I require it, and at the hand of man; at the hand of every man's brother will I require the life of man. Whoso sheddeth man's blood, by man shall his blood be shed: for in the image of God made he man.

> And you, be ye fruitful, and multiply; bring forth abundantly in the earth, and multiply therein.
>
> And God spake unto Noah, and to his sons with him, saying, And I, behold, I establish my covenant with you, and with your seed after you; And with every living creature that is with you, of the fowl, of the cattle, and of every beast of the earth with you; from all that go out of the ark, to every beast of the earth. And I will establish my covenant with you; neither shall all flesh be cut off any more by the waters of a flood; neither shall there any more be a flood to destroy the earth. And God said, This is the token of the covenant which I make between me and you and every living creature that is with you, for perpetual generations: I do set my bow in the cloud, and it shall be for a token of a covenant between me and the earth. And it shall come to pass, when I bring a cloud over the earth, that the bow shall be seen in the cloud: And I will remember my covenant, which is between me and you and every living creature of all flesh; and the waters shall no more become a flood to destroy all flesh. And the bow shall be in the cloud; and I will look upon it, that I may remember the everlasting covenant between God and every living creature of all flesh that is upon the earth. And God said unto Noah, This is the token of the covenant, which I have established between me and all flesh that is upon the earth. (Gen 9:1-17)

I have purposely repeated the first 17 verses of Chapter 9 here; I wish that nothing be taken out of context. Firstly, God commanded Noah and his sons to "be fruitful, and multiply, and replenish the earth". This is basically the same command that He gave to Adam with one important omission. In Genesis 1:28, God issued these commands along with the command to "subdue it" (i.e., the earth) and to "rule" over it. Noah was not given this command.

Obviously, man was no longer the "king" of the earth because he was, now, not able to subdue it.

Before the Flood, all the animals were vegetarians; now many were carnivores. Just as Noah was now allowed to eat meat, so were the animals. Some of the animals were so huge, swift, stealthy, and powerful that God had to supernaturally protect man from them by placing a latent fear of man in them. If you've ever wondered why animals usually choose to avoid man and run from him, here is the reason.

Secondly, this age begins with God's words, "Whoso sheddeth man's blood, by man shall his blood be shed." Obviously before the Flood, chaos reigned. Men were committing all kinds of atrocities against each other with impunity. Stephen Quayle, in Genesis 6 Giants, relates the stories, recorded by the ancients, that the giants were actually cannibalistic. God now gave instructions to Noah, and his family, that men could judge acts of evil committed against others. Even though this statement seems to limit man to only reserve judgment against murder, the implications are more far-reaching. By these instructions, God gave His authority to man to set up governments to institutionalize definitions of crime and punishment and to act upon these definitions. Governments were originally set up as city-states; each city having its own laws. Each city was originally founded by family groups who agreed to abide by these laws. As these city-states grew, strangers would either settle permanently or temporarily in the city-state and be forced to abide by the laws governing the city-state. Also as generations passed, new laws were passed or old ones changed to the point of alienating the government, and its laws, from the people. Thus, governments became more and more powerful and removed from the interests of the people. Many became monarchies. Monarchies would eventually become imperialistic and expand to overtake weaker city-states. So many of these petty "kings" emerged that, eventually, the concept of nations was formed that included many cities.

Thirdly, God established a **Covenant** between Himself and Noah, his sons, and all flesh. This Covenant promised that God would no longer destroy the earth with a worldwide flood. As a sign to the earth's inhabitants and a remembrance of His Covenant, God would cause a rainbow to form in the sky after a rainfall. What is a covenant? A covenant is simply a promise. In the Bible, God makes only two kinds of covenants: conditional and unconditional. A conditional covenant means that God will only keep His promise dependent on some conditional act of the one(s) God is making the promise to. In a way, eating of the forbidden fruit by Adam and Eve was a conditional covenant (although a negative one): the day they ate of the fruit they would die. The opposite is obviously true: they would never die if they hadn't partaken of the fruit. An unconditional covenant is a promise that God makes that is incumbent upon only Himself to fulfill. The rainbow is a good example of an unconditional covenant; mankind is not required to do anything for God to never send another worldwide flood. Sometimes Godly covenants can be very difficult to determine whether they are conditional or unconditional. This is a serious matter, for the conditionality of God's covenants clearly affects the future. We shall try, in the rest of this text, to determine, honestly, the conditionality of God's covenants.

The Post-Flood World

That the postdiluvian world was radically different from the antediluvian world should be obvious. As we have touched upon in the last chapter, there are marked changes in the postdiluvian environment. We should, however, firstly address one of the more important aspects of the Flood as recorded in the biblical record. The Bible states:

> **And the ark rested in the seventh month, on the seventeenth day of the month, upon the mountains of Ararat. (Gen 8:4)**

Please notice that the Bible states that the ark rested on the mountains of Ararat. According to most biblical scholars, this translation should not be taken quite so literally because many proper names have changed since the Flood, and Ararat is certainly one of them. Many books have been written, in recent years, that a knot of mountains located in present day Turkey and near the country of Armenia has two special mountains within it called Lesser Ararat and Greater Ararat. Known mostly by people in the nearby vicinities there is, supposedly, an ancient sea vessel, made entirely of wood, located on an almost inaccessible glacier on Greater Ararat. Only during the longest hot and dry stretches of the year is this boat accessible. It has been reported that this boat has been visited by many ancient explorers, and has the dimensions of Noah's ark as recorded in the Bible. Because of the political situation between Russia and Turkey, Greater Ararat's inhospitable climate, and the location of the ark on the glacier at approximately 13,000 feet (close to the summit of 17,000 feet), recent expeditions have been costly, diplomatic, and very difficult to organize. Furthermore, some of the tribes in the area have never been completely civilized and remain hostile to outsiders, and some expeditions have disappeared without a trace. Those expeditions that have been successful have been written about fairly extensively in such books as John Warwick Montgomery's The Quest for Noah's Ark. Pieces of the boat have been taken by some explorers and carbon dated. The dates determined from the wood fragments agree wonderfully with our and Bishop Ussher's chronology.

Even though I have excoriated carbon-14 dating previously, I must make an exception here. The half-life of Carbon-14 is 5,730 years depending on wich reference is consulted. Carbon-14 dating, when used for dating ancient things such as fossils, requires many occurrences of the half-life of the radioactive carbon. Each time the half-life is calculated, it increases the errors that come with the calculations. Thus, things that are supposedly millions of years old have compounded these errors immeasurably. Younger things, within about one or two half-lifes, may still have errors present in their dating scheme but not so terribly that the dating can't be approximated sufficiently to within a thousand years or so. As an example, let's take two sets of data and call them set A and set B. Because these two sets have more data than can be counted, we take statistical samples. We find that set A measures 6 with a possible error of plus or minus 1. Set B measures 5 also with a possible error of plus or minus 1. If we were to add the sets together, set A would contribute 5 to 7 and set B would contribute 4 to 6 because of the possible errors. This would result in 11 with a plus or minus error of 2. This new result would then be anywhere from 9 to 13. If, however, we were to *multiply* the two sets, we would get anywhere from 20 to 42 with the most likely result of 6*5 = 30. We'd get 20 because it is possible that either set could be the lowest possible numbers of 5 and 4 and 5*4 = 20. Likewise, the highest possible numbers of 7 and 6 would yield 7*6 = 42. Thus, our new measurements would yield a number of 30 with a possible plus error of 12 and a possible minus error of 10! So it's easy to see how quickly these errors accrue.

Bob Cornuke, a biblical explorer, has disagreed with the "traditional" location of Noah's Ark. Based on ancient maps, there was once a nation that is now incorporated in the northwest corner of modern day Iran that was called "Urartu". There was a mountain chain in the northern part of this nation called the Urartu Mountains. Translated into modern English, Urartu becomes Ararat! To this day, Bob has made only one unsuccessful expedition to a mountain in Iran, which is traditionally known as the mountain of Noah by the local population. According to Mr. Cornuke, this mountain makes a lot more sense as the landing site of Noah because of its accessibility, the easier transition down the mountain for Noah, his family, and the animals, etc. Bob Cornuke and David Halbrook have written a book about this expedition entitled The Lost Mountain of Noah. This book is a *must* read for the serious Bible student.

It is quite probable that, as this book goes to press, Noah's Ark may have finally been discovered on Mt. Suleiman (Solomon) in northern Iran. In the June, 2010 edition of the magazine, Prophecy in the News, an article entitled Has Noah's Ark Been Found at Last? documents a discovery by Arch Bonnema of a large, wooden boat on the mountain at an elevation of 13,126 feet. All of the wood has long since been petrified, but other finds include animal hair from tigers and lions, butterfly wings from butterflies that are only found in South America today, barnacles on the wood, and petrified sea anemones. For more information on this discovery, please see the article alluded to here.

We have already alluded to the longevity of the patriarchs (oldest living persons recorded about). Again after the Flood, we have reasonably recorded evidence of these supposed long ages that we can scrutinize scientifically. Beginning with Noah and his three sons' ages, we can see if we can map the ages recorded in the Bible to a mathematical function. If we can, then natural processes can be seen to be at work to reduce the upper limit of 1,000 years of the antediluvian patriarchs to the upper limit of 120 years of the postdiluvian patriarchs.

> **And the LORD said, My spirit shall not always strive with man, for that he also is flesh: yet his days shall be an hundred and twenty years. (Gen 6:3)**

That this quotation refers to man's maximum possible lifespan after the Flood is a highly debated issue. I, for one, believe it. It is hotly debated because, in context, it refers to how long the antediluvian world had to repent before God sent the Flood since this is the length of time Noah took to build the ark. It could also serve the double purpose of prophesying the maximum lifespan of mankind. Getting back to the analysis of the patriarchal lifespans, Joseph C. Dillow, in his masterful work entitled The Waters Above, begins his analysis with Noah's recorded lifespan and traces the ages of all the patriarchal lifespans down to Moses. Since Noah and Shem lived before the Flood, it is more scientifically accurate to calculate a regression analysis from Arpachshad to Moses and to disregard the ages of Noah and Shem. Arpachshad, significantly, was the first child born after the Flood; he was born two years after. Performing his statistical analysis, he does what is called a "linear regression" and comes up with:

$$Y = 436e^{-0.119x}$$

where Y is the patriarch's age at death and x is the number of generations after Arpachshad – Arpachshad's generation being 0. Dr. Dillow then calculated a "correlation coefficient" for his linear regression and resulting mathematical equation. To explain, a linear regression takes points on a piece of graph paper and calculates the closest mathematical equation that will fit the points. In this way, a straight line is drawn that most closely fits the points. The points in this calculation are the patriarchal ages from Noah to Moses. This, however, is not enough because the points could be scattered all over the graph paper and the mathematical equation, which one is almost sure to get from the linear regression, may not be a very good approximation to the points. The closer the points are to the equation or line, the better the "fit". A correlation coefficient calculates the distances the points are from what the equation predicts and performs a calculation to determine how well the points predict the equation. A correlation coefficient of 0 shows absolutely no correlation between the points, and a correlation coefficient of 1 shows that all the points are exactly on the line drawn by the equation. A fit of .7 is considered a fairly good fit. Dr. Dillow, however, calculated a correlation coefficient of .94! Because this correlation is so high, the points graphed show that this mathematical equation is a very likely predictor of the patriarchal ages after the Flood; and, in turn, it shows a great deal of likelihood that natural processes were at work (especially the fact that the points on the graph were distributed randomly on either side of the line showing natural randomness). This, then, lends scientific credence to the literality of the biblical record, that Noah's Flood was an historical reality, that Bishop Ussher's chronology must be accorded its due respect, and that these patriarchs were true, literal people! Based on Bishop Ussher's chronology, Dr. Dillow calculates a date of 2346 B.C. for the Flood.

The Table of Nations

Genesis Chapter 10 has come to be called the "Table of Nations" by many archaeologists. This chapter records the genealogies of Noah's sons: Shem, Ham, and Japheth. Also recorded in this chapter, to some degree, is the geographical point of settlement of many of these offspring. Many of these places have been discovered, dug up, and references found to the original founder of the settlement. The original founders have been verified to be the very same people as identified in the Bible. For example, the oldest obelisk found in Egypt had the words "The Land of

Ham" inscribed on it. Because of this, many archaeologists have accorded the written record of the Bible the respect it deserves.

Ham's descendants mainly settled in the Mideast and modern Africa. Shem's descendants mainly stayed in the Mideast. Japheth's descendants seemed to move north and west of the Mideast settling in today's modern Europe and Asia. Because the descendants of each of Noah's sons isolated themselves from each other geographically, the gene pools of Noah's sons did not normally intermix. Many scholars consider this non-intermixing of the gene pools the origin of today's races. Ham and his sons were very possibly black. Shem and his sons were probably the brown peoples that populate the modern Mideast. Japheth and his sons were probably the white peoples that inhabit modern Europe. The oriental people's origins are still hotly debated today. Some contend that they are descendants of Japheth, and some claim they are descended from Ham.

Nimrod

We have purposely set aside a separate section of this Dispensation to discuss Nimrod. Even though the Bible seems to mention Nimrod passingly, the very fact that he is accorded three verses in the Scriptures points to the fact that he must have been a very important historical figure indeed.

> **And Cush begat Nimrod: he began to be a mighty one in the earth. He was a mighty hunter before the LORD: wherefore it is said, Even as Nimrod the mighty hunter before the LORD. And the beginning of his kingdom was Babel, and Erech, and Accad, and Calneh, in the land of Shinar. (Gen 10:8-10)**

Please notice that Nimrod was descended from Cush who was, in turn, descended from Ham. Also, Cush's wife, as usual, is not mentioned. We present here a very important question: was Nimrod a Nephilim? That is, was he the product of an unlawful intermingling between Cush's wife and an angel? In his excellent book, The Two Babylons, Alexander Hislop draws some very interesting conclusions from known archaeological evidence. We must understand, here, that Hislop's main motive, in writing his book, is to attach pagan practices to the Roman Catholic Church, and, as such, his discussion of Nimrod is given only the space necessary to address his influence on these practices.

Most biblical scholars agree with Hislop that the biblical phrase, "He was a mighty hunter before the Lord", is a negative reference. This reference has absolutely nothing to do with hunting game; he also hunted men. Hislop claims that Nimrod was a giant. His gigantic stature made him feared. This he used to his advantage. Furthermore, his strength was legendary. Antiquity accords him the fame of killing a bull with his bare hands, removing the bull's horns, and then wearing them. This gave the king's crown its symbolism; each horn on the crown represented power; the more horns one had on his crown, the greater was his power. Over the years the pictures uncovered of Nimrod went gradually from depicting Nimrod with the bull's horns to eventually portraying him with the bull's hind legs and tail. This, according to Hislop, is where we get today's pictorial portrayal of Satan!

According to Hislop, Nimrod wished to rule a worldwide government from the place he founded: Babel. Please notice the biblical reference we've just quoted specifying this. Nimrod used fear and strength to get the earth's inhabitants to obey him. Those who disobeyed, he hunted and killed. But Nimrod was no dummy. He knew he couldn't coerce the entire world to follow him through fear alone. So what he did was to marry a blonde-haired, blue-eyed beauty named Semiramis. Unfortunately, she was even more evil and cunning than he. She instituted a pagan religion and convinced most of the world to follow it.

This religion, that the Bible continually refers to as Babylon, was begun under the auspices of the Protevangelium (Gen. 3:15) that we've alluded to earlier. The stars, which could now be clearly seen after the Flood, were mapped into constellations. These constellations, taken in the correct order, told the story of the Protevangelium (take a closer look at them some time). After Nimrod and Semiramis had a son, called Tammuz, Semiramis claimed that Tammuz was virgin-born and that she was the mother, or queen, of heaven. Sound familiar? Tammuz, then, was the long-awaited savior that the world expected. She changed the story of the Protevangelium in the constellations to downright worship of the stars. This is the origin of today's astrology. Her religion, in order to add to its appeal, was described in various symbols and rites. These various symbols and rites supposedly had very mysterious meanings that only the adept could learn. The ecclesiastical construction of the religion of Babylon was built upon the notion of circles within circles. The most outward circle was reserved for those who believed, in pure faith, that the priests of religious Babylon knew the true meanings of these symbols and rites, communicated with God, and honestly represented God to man. The gradual increase in knowledge of the symbols and rites qualified one to advance gradually towards the inner circles. But to advance from an outward circle to an inner circle, the adherent had to confess his sins to a member of the inner circle. Each time a smaller, inner circle was to be advanced into, the aspirant's confessions had to reveal more and more "dirt" about himself. If the ambitious aspirant, after advancing to ever-inner circles, were to wake up and discover that the symbols and rites were meaningless shams, his "confessions" would keep him from publishing his revelations for fear that his "sins" would be exposed to the public!

Hislop's work is truly revealing. His book contains photographs of statues, steles, and pictures uncovered archaeologically that "prove" his assertions. For example, archaeology has unearthed many statues of "Madonna and child" from various points across the globe. Many of these places make no claim of believing in Christianity and actually predate Mary and Jesus. How, then, can they possibly be explained except on his assertion that these "idols" represented Semiramis' religion and was worldwide after the people dispersed after the Tower of Babel Judgment.

The Tower of Babel

The Dispensation of Government ended with God's confusion of tongues and the dispersal of people all over the world from the Tower of Babel. This is addressed in Genesis Chapter 11, verses 1 to 9, which we shall not repeat here. One thing is worthy, however, of discussion about the Tower of Babel. Ancient stories seem to relate that the Tower was Nimrod's symbol of world unity. Recent scholars have dug up evidence that the Tower was actually a **ziggurat** used by the ancients to worship the stars. If this is so, the Tower was actually being constructed for Semiramis' religion.

How did Nimrod and Semiramis meet their ends? There are no known ancient legends that I know of that relate to Semiramis' demise; but the ancient legends are replete with tales of how Nimrod eventually died. One of these legends I shall repeat here. Supposedly, Shem, who was still alive during this fiasco, gathered some of his closest friends together and hunted Nimrod down. What a switch! The man who hunted other men was now, himself, hunted! When he was caught, Shem executed him, cut his body into small pieces, and sent the pieces to the other leaders of the world as a reminder of what could happen to them if they, in turn, contemplated the same kind of mischief that Nimrod attempted.

As a passing mention, we must remark that God ended this dispensation because man failed at government. How so? Man attempted to construct a global government. God did not wish this because mankind would be united in its attempt to defy God.

> And the LORD said, Behold, the people is one, and they have all one language; and this they begin to do: and now nothing will be restrained from them, which they have imagined to do. (Gen 11:6)

God does not want mankind to be united in his evil. Please notice the phrase, "nothing will be restrained from them, which they have imagined to do." Instead of city-states competing in their governmental structures to continually attract new citizens, they were uniting in one, global, conglomerate government. God knows that once people unite in a common cause apart from Him, the result, with man, can only be evil. This situation He will allow for Lucifer but only at the right time. Dispensation 3 was obviously not the right time! There is, however, a strong push for world government in our day. So, we ask you: is today's drive towards globalism good or evil?

Chapter 7

DISPENSATION 4: PROMISE

This Dispensation is marked by God's call to Abram and His Promise to him. This Age is covered by Genesis Chapter 12 through Exodus Chapter 19. Since the story of the Tower of Babel is given no timeline, we cannot tell if Abram's call came immediately after the confusion of tongues. Knowing God, His Purposes, and His Love for mankind, we find it hard to believe that God would allow men to walk the earth without an immediately new Revelation from Him.

Abram's call came in Genesis Chapter 12:

> Now the LORD had said unto Abram, Get thee out of thy country, and from thy kindred, and from thy father's house, unto a land that I will shew thee: And I will make of thee a great nation, and I will bless thee, and make thy name great; and thou shalt be a blessing: And I will bless them that bless thee, and curse him that curseth thee: and in thee shall all families of the earth be blessed. (Gen 12:1-3)

At this time in history, people were still wandering across the face of the known world and settling down in new areas. Some, who were responsible for building new civilizations, were successful, and some were unsuccessful. God's covenant with Abram promised him success if he would settle in the land that God had called him to. This was obviously a conditional covenant in that it required that Abram follow God's call to settle, with his wife Sarai, in a land that God would specify.

God called Abram from a city-state known as Ur of the Chaldees.

> **And Terah took Abram his son, and Lot the son of Haran his son's son, and Sarai his daughter in law, his son Abram's wife; and they went forth with them from Ur of the Chaldees, to go into the land of Canaan; and they came unto Haran, and dwelt there. (Gen 11:31)**

Archaeologists have recently found the city-state of Ur and discovered many interesting things about it. First of all, it was a large, well-known, and thriving city-state. It was well ordered in that trade, religion, education, etc. were advanced for the times. It was as civilized a place as existed. Thus, God's call required Abram to leave a very settled, civilized existence, away from home and family, and travel to some unknown land. This, obviously, required a great deal of faith in God!

Please notice that this passage seems to say that Abram was not actually called out of Ur but out of Haran where his father Terah settled. Now, Nelson's Bible Dictionary says of Haran:

> HARAN
>
> [HAIR uhn] (meaning unknown)-- the name of three men and one city in the Old Testament:
>
> 1. The third son of Terah, Abraham's father, and the younger brother of Abraham. Haran was the father of Lot, Milcah, and Iscah <Gen. 11:26-31>.
>
> 2. A city of northern Mesopotamia where Abraham and his father Terah lived for a time

> <Gen. 11:31-32; 12:4-5>. The family of Abraham's brother Nahor also lived in this city for a time, as did Jacob and his wife Rachel <Gen. 28:10; 29:4-5>. The city was on the Balikh, a tributary of the Euphrates River, 386 kilometers (240 miles) northwest of Nineveh and 450 kilometers (280 miles) northeast of Damascus. Haran lay on one of the main trade routes between Babylonia and the Mediterranean Sea. Like the inhabitants of Ur of the Chaldees, Haran's inhabitants worshiped Sin, the moon-god. <Second Kings 19:12> records that the city was captured by the Assyrians. Today Haran is a small Arab village, Harran. Haran is also spelled as Charran <Acts 7:2,4>; (KJV).
>
> 3. A son of Caleb by Ephah, Caleb's concubine. Haran was the father of Gazez <1 Chr. 2:46>.
>
> 4. A Levite from the family of Gershon and a son of Shimei. Haran lived during David's reign <1 Chr. 23:9>.

Notice, in particular, reference 2. This describes the ancient city which, obviously, still exists today. Many scholars believe that the call of Abram (Gen 12:1-3) is a repeat call that was originally given to him when he lived in Ur. Remember, however, what we've already discussed about the ancient Hebrew language; it is not necessarily concerned with chronology. Moreover, Moses seems to accord Terah the reverence owed him as Abram's father because he (Moses) says that Terah led the family from Ur. Because of other biblical references to Abram's call (Neh 9:7, Isa 51:2, Acts 7:2-4), Abram was the one called out of Ur. He was not called, at least originally, from Haran! God, in His infinite justice and wisdom, gives full credit to Abram, not Terah, for obeying the divine call because Abram continued on to the land which God had chosen!

> **By faith Abraham, when he was called to go out into a place which he should after receive for an inheritance, obeyed; and he went out, not knowing whither he went. (Heb 11:8)**

There are many other passages in the Scriptures that discuss Abram's faith. Some of the more interesting ones include Abram's name change to Abraham (Gen 17:5), Abraham's and Sarah's (Sarai's name was changed too) conception in old age (Gen 21:2-3), the birth of Ishmael through Hagar (Gen 16:3,15), Abraham's tribute to Melchizedek (Gen 14:18-20), Abraham's questions to God about the righteous living in Sodom before He pored Judgment upon it (Gen 18:23-32), Abraham's dutiful response to God's command to sacrifice his son Isaac (Gen 22: 1-19), circumcision instituted among Abraham's seed (Gen 17:10-14), etc. In the New Testament Book of Hebrews, God gives full credit to the faith of Abraham. What a man Abraham must've been! Listen, now, to the voice of God:

> **And he believed in the LORD; and he counted it to him for righteousness. (Gen 15:6)**

Anyone, to whom the Lord imputes (counts as) righteousness, is saved! This is because righteousness implies sinlessness, which is, in effect, salvation because all mortal men are sinners. Thus, salvation is, in other words, a simple decree issued by God. Abraham, therefore, was saved by definition!

Doctor J. R. Church, in his wonderful magazine Prophecy in the News, has studied the Hebrew language in depth and has come up with an interesting observation. The Hebrew letter hay, the equivalent to "h" in English, has one special, symbolic meaning. It is symbolic of the Holy Spirit. Once God adds an "hay" to someone's name, it means that the Holy Spirit now dwells with that person! The indwelling of the Holy Spirit is exactly what happens to those who are saved during Dispensation 6, the Church Age. Please notice that Abram's and Sarai's names were changed to Abraham and Sarah respectively: the addition of an "hay" to their names in the Hebrew!

One other thing, about God's covenant with Abraham, deserves special mention. After Abraham obeyed God's original call to move to Canaan, God's promises were now incumbent upon Him alone; that is, God's promises to Abraham were now unconditional:

> And he said unto him, I am the LORD that brought thee out of Ur of the Chaldees, to give thee this land to inherit it. And he said, Lord GOD, whereby shall I know that I shall inherit it? And he said unto him, Take me an heifer of three years old, and a she goat of three years old, and a ram of three years old, and a turtledove, and a young pigeon. And he took unto him all these, and divided them in the midst, and laid each piece one against another: but the birds divided he not. And when the fowls came down upon the carcases, Abram drove them away. And when the sun was going down, a deep sleep fell upon Abram; and, lo, an horror of great darkness fell upon him. And he said unto Abram, Know of a surety that thy seed shall be a stranger in a land that is not theirs, and shall serve them; and they shall afflict them four hundred years; And also that nation, whom they shall serve, will I judge: and afterward shall they come out with great substance. And thou shalt go to thy fathers in peace; thou shalt be buried in a good old age. But in the fourth generation they shall come hither again: for the iniquity of the Amorites is not yet full. And it came to pass, that, when the sun went down, and it was dark, behold a smoking furnace, and a burning lamp that passed between those pieces.
>
> In the same day the LORD made a covenant with Abram, saying, Unto thy seed have I given this land, from the river of Egypt unto the great river, the river Euphrates: The Kenites, and the Kenizzites, and the Kadmonites, And the Hittites, and the Perizzites, and the Rephaims, And the Amorites, and the Canaanites, and the Girgashites, and the Jebusites. (Gen 15:7-21)

This is an amazing passage of Scripture! When God repeated and expounded His, now, unconditional covenant with Abraham, He symbolically took a "blood oath" to keep it. Scholars have discovered that, during Abraham's day, a blood oath was an agreement made, usually, between the leaders of two clans. The agreement could be one against the mutual encroachment of each other's land, war, intermarriage, etc. It was called a blood oath because to break it meant the promise of the offending party's agreement to let the other kill him. To symbolically bind the parties, each would take animals, cut them in pieces, lay the pieces in parallel lines across from each other, and the two parties would each, in turn, pass between the rows of mutilated animals. Once done, the blood oath was sealed. In this passage of Scripture, Abraham asks God, in humility, how he could know that God would keep his promises. God then instructs Abraham to lay out the mutilated pieces of animals in parallel rows symbolically as a blood oath. God then causes Abraham to fall into a deep sleep and passes between the rows Himself ("a smoking furnace, and a burning lamp")! The reference to the smoking furnace and burning lamp are obvious references to God, Himself, as God appeared to the Jews, in the wilderness and later, as the Shekinah Glory. If this is not proof positive that this covenant is now unconditional, we don't know how God could've made it any plainer. Has this covenant ever been fulfilled? We don't believe so because God swore that Abraham's descendants would occupy the land from "the river of Egypt" to "the great river Euphrates". Even though scholars are not in agreement as to the identity of "the river of Egypt", the Euphrates River has been a constant since ancient times to this day. This land was promised, once again, to Abraham's descendants. Which ones, Jacob's, Esau's, or Ishmael's? We believe that only the children of God's inheritance, the Jews, were made this promise. Why? Because once Ishmael and Esau left the camp, the Bible only makes passing references to them. Jacob's seed is traced throughout the pages of the rest of Scripture. We, therefore, believe that God has not as yet fulfilled His promises to the Jews, the seed of Jacob.

The covenant that God made with Abraham is known as the **Abrahamic Covenant**. Understanding God's covenants are just as important to understanding the Bible as the Dispensational Theory. Important, but less in significance, is the Noahic covenant and others. Two of the more important covenants are the Davidic Covenant and the New Covenant. We shall address these as we encounter them chronologically.

Abraham's obedience to God's call set up a new approach to God's Plan of Redemption. From here on, God would pass His "inheritance" through individuals. What was God's inheritance? It was a promise that one's descendant would inherit what Adam originally forfeited - King of the Earth! As we trace this through, we will understand more about this. For now and this dispensation, suffice it to say that God passed His inheritance through Abraham, Isaac, Jacob (later renamed Israel), and Jacob's twelve sons (the Jews).

Why the Jews? Why not someone else or no one in particular? Because of the Abrahamic Covenant! God promised Abraham that His Plan of Redemption would now be passed through Abraham's seed. The descendants of Abraham, Isaac, and Jacob are called Jews. The reason that God called out a particular people to carry out His Plan was to identify one race, or ethnic group, with whom He could directly communicate.

> **What advantage then hath the Jew? or what profit is there of circumcision? Much every way: chiefly, because that unto them were committed the oracles of God. (Rom 3:1-2)**

As an example of God's oracles being passed to the Jews, only two books of the Bible may have been written by non-Jews (Luke: Luke and Acts). I sincerely believe that Luke, once more of his ethnic background is discovered, will turn out to be a Jew also. Furthermore, God would use the Jewish seed to be the line through which the promised seed (remember, the Protevangelium) would be born as the Savior to all mankind. More will be said about this subject matter in the next chapter.

One other thing must be addressed before we leave this dispensation - the reference in the biblical passage quoted to the Amorites. God said that there would be four generations before the iniquity of the Amorites was full. The Amorites were a tribe of people who inhabited Canaan side-by-side with Abraham. That the four generations that would pass until their evil was full is understood by biblical scholars as the length of time until God freed the Jews of their enslavement in Egypt. The beginning of the countdown of the four generations, however, is highly controversial. In some passages of Scripture, the Bible seems to refer to 430 years as the length of time the Jews were enslaved in Egypt. In other passages, different lengths of time are given. The main question here is whether the passages referred to are counting from the time of God's statement, the length of time the Jews were in Egypt, or the length of time the Jews were enslaved. Whatever duration is correct, we cannot honestly say. But, as we shall see, the judgment of the Amorites, and other tribes, were performed by the Jews (for God).

Whether this dispensation ends with the enslavement of the Jews in Egypt, their wanderings in the wilderness, or whatever is very difficult to determine. Again, biblical scholars are in disagreement over this issue. Because we believe that God is a God of order, both logically and chronologically, we must end this dispensation with the enslavement of the Jews in the land of Egypt. Why? Because of when we wish to begin God's next dispensation.

Chapter 8

DISPENSATION 5: LAW

We believe that God began His fifth dispensation with His giving of the **Ten Commandments** at Mt. Sinai. This Age is covered from Exodus Chapter 20 through the rest of the Old Testament. From here on, God would no longer leave man's obedience up to man's conscience, responsibilities, morals, judgment, etc.; but He would clearly define those acts which were disobedient to Him. The Ten Commandments were merely the beginning of the **Law**. The Jews, whom He adopted as His own people, were given other commandments which must also be obeyed. Scholars have counted the number of commandments that God gave the Jews to obey. Some have come up with the incredible number of 613 of them! This is the number we shall use. There was, however, one glitch to the Law - disobedience to any one of them, at any time, was tantamount to disobedience to all of them. Because God is perfect, He cannot tolerate one simple act of disobedience. Thus, one could assure one's future salvation, and eternal life, by perfect obedience to the Law; by the same token, one would definitely lose his salvation through disobedience. There are many references in the Bible concerning this:

> For whosoever shall keep the whole law, and yet offend in one point, he is guilty of all. (James 2:10)

Why, in the world, would God give men so many, and such complicated, laws that they couldn't possibly obey? This topic will be treated fully when we come to the next dispensation.

But, does God know man? You bet He does! As a means for covering offenses (sin), God instituted animal sacrifices. There were a lot of sacrifices that could be performed to cover various sins. But, you might say, why would God have the Jews perform the bloody deed of sacrificing innocent animals to atone for their mistakes? There is one good reason which we shall cover shortly.

Theocracy

When God "married" the Jews at Mt. Sinai in the wilderness, He set up the Jews as a special nation. They were to be answerable only to Him. Thus, *God* was their king. This is the meaning of the word **Theocracy**. They were to distribute God's laws to other nations across the world and thereby convert other nations to God and His ways. God specifically told the Jewish nation that if they weren't obedient to Him, He would wrest their divine blessings and privileges and send them, as a nation, into captivity into a foreign land.

> Because thou servedst not the LORD thy God with joyfulness, and with gladness of heart, for the abundance of all things; Therefore shalt thou serve thine enemies which the LORD shall send against thee, in hunger, and in thirst, and in nakedness, and in want of all things: and he shall put a yoke of iron upon thy neck, until he have destroyed thee. The LORD shall bring a nation against thee from far, from the end of the earth, as swift as the eagle flieth; a nation whose tongue thou shalt not understand; A nation of fierce countenance, which shall not regard the person of the old, nor shew favour to the young: (Deut 28:47-50)

These verses should suffice to prove our point.

In His Theocracy, God specified three important stations: prophet, priest, and king. A prophet was one who communicated God's Word to whomever it was intended. This included prophecies. A priest was one who communicated men's needs to God and performed sacrifices for men's sins. A king was one who ruled over the people in God's will. At the earliest stages of His Theocracy, God, once again, was the king.

As a passing comment, we must remember that the Jews are God's people. They are not His people because of ethnicity, race, religion, etc.; but simply because they are the children of faithful Abraham. God's promises were repeated to Isaac and Jacob and then to Jacob's (i.e., Israel's) 12 sons. Regardless of the Jews' continual disobedience that God foreknew would occur, God made a blood oath with Abraham. Since the promises to Abraham have never been realized, we maintain, that because God keeps His Word (an unconditional covenant), someday they will be realized.

This dispensation clearly includes the nation of Israel's history. Upon entering the land of Canaan (present day Palestine) God had Joshua clear the land for the Jewish settlers. In many cases Joshua was instructed by God to kill men, women, children, and animals in some cities. This seems to be a cruel act for a merciful God. If we remember the report of the Jewish spies who went ahead to scout the land before the Jews entered:

> And they brought up an evil report of the land which they had searched unto the children of Israel, saying, The land, through which we have gone to search it, is a land that eateth up the inhabitants thereof; and all the people that we saw in it are men of a great stature. And there we saw the giants, the sons of Anak, which come of the giants: and we were in our own sight as grasshoppers, and so we were in their sight. (Num 13:32-33)

Giants, again! Could these giants be Nephilim? You bet! It is the same Hebrew word found back in Genesis Chapter 6. Satan was up to the same old tricks that he used before in the antediluvian world. Stephen Quayle, in his book Genesis 6 Giants, demonstrates that many ancient civilizations faced opposition from giants dwelling in remote corners of the earth. Whether this is true or not, God obviously allowed Satan the chance to thwart His plans in building up the military might of the land's inhabitants. If the Jews were too weak or too afraid to enter the land, God's promises to the Jews would never be realized. Then a Deliverer would not come for the world. But Satan didn't count on God's help! This is the very reason that God punished the Jews with their 40-year wanderings in the wilderness when they refused to enter the land. After all, God, Himself, had promised to help them to conquer the Promised Land!

Another small mention must be made of the Nephilim in the land of Canaan. Please notice that God allowed the Amorites to fill up their own wickedness. In the antediluvian world, the biblical passages suggest that the "daughters of men" were taken by the "sons of God" as they chose. This implies force. The women in the antediluvian world were possibly forced to cohabit with the fallen angels. In these passages, God allowed the inhabitants of Canaan to behave wickedly. This implies free will. Also notice in particular, that the sons of one particular man, Anak, were Nephilim. Not everyone in Canaan cohabited with the fallen angels; it seemed to run in families. Archaeologists have uncovered stories from the Middle East concerning incubi and succubi. Incubi are supposedly male spirits who come around in the night to offer cohabitation with women, and succubi are the female counterparts. According to ancient literature, many of the civilizations in the Middle East suffered from these nightly visitors. Happily, the ancients mostly feared them, or the plague of the Nephilim would have been much more widespread. Believe it or not, these nightly visitors still make their appearances today mostly in the more pagan parts of the world.

The Wilderness

Before entering the Promised Land, God had the Jews gather at Mt. Sinai. From Mt. Sinai and the giving of the Ten Commandments, God set up standards for the Jews. Each tribe was given its own insignia, nickname, and geographical place in relation to the other tribes. The insignia and nicknames were pretty much in accordance with Jacob's (i.e., Israel's) prophecies concerning the 12 tribes (Gen 49). A very interesting book written by William Varner, entitled Jacob's Dozen, goes into some detail about Jacob's prophecies. The prophecy given to Dan is, possibly, very telling. The relative locations of the tribes were done to show the relative locations of the tribes' locations when they occupied the Promised Land. Because the entire tribe of Levi sided with God against the rebellion at Mt. Sinai, they were rewarded with the perpetual role of priests. They were given no land because they, as priests and predisposed to administering to the whole house of Israel, had to be located throughout the land. Their land was given to Joseph who, in turn, divided his land between his two sons: Manasseh and Ephraim to keep the number of tribes that were allotted land at the constant number of 12.

As another interesting aside, the true Mount Sinai has been discovered by Bob Cornuke. It's not on the Sinai Peninsula as has been historically believed; it's in Saudi Arabia! The video The Search for the Real Mt. Sinai by Robert Cornuke and Larry Williams shows the features around the mountain that the Bible describes. They've discovered the bitter waters of Marah (Ex. 15:23), where Moses struck the rock to release the water (Ex. 17:6), and other things that prove that they've actually discovered the Jews' flight path from Egypt. What is most interesting is that the Saudis have this area fenced off and patrolled by armed guards. In other words, these "Muslims" *know* the truth of the Bible and are hiding it from their subjects! Please see this video.

God required the Jews to enter Palestine from the eastern end of the Sinai Peninsula because the western end was heavily defended by many nations including the Egyptians. The western end of Sinai was a major trade route between the nations. Once reaching the border of Palestine at the Jordan River, God required Moses to delegate a spy from each tribe to search out the Promised Land. The 12 spies were gone 40 days. Upon their return, only Joshua and Caleb had the courage and faith to make a positive report that the land, with God's help, could be taken. The others, reporting the presence of giants in the land, were afraid that the Jews lacked the necessary might to take the land. The rest of the camp sided with the 10 unfaithful spies. God, Who had performed miracles on the Jews' behalf, became angry with them and cursed everyone. With the exceptions of Joshua and Caleb, everyone over 20 years old was to never inhabit the promised land. To accomplish this, He had the Jews wander aimlessly in the desert of Sinai (i.e., the wilderness) one year for each day the spies were in the land. Thus, the Jews wandered in the desert for 40 years until the whole, unfaithful generation died off. This whole story is told in Numbers Chapters 13 and 14.

The Shekinah Glory Cloud

In the story of the Jews' exodus from Egypt, a pillar of fire separated the Egyptians from the Jews. Interestingly rather than to dissipate, the Jews were told by Moses that this pillar of fire was the very presence of God. It led the Jews in their travels by appearing as a cloud by day and a pillar of fire by night. That there really could have been a Shekinah Glory Cloud is explained naturalistically by Immanuel Velikovsky in Worlds in Collision.

The Tabernacle

Because of their wanderings but also because God required special worship from them, the Jews were instructed to build a transportable House of God. Called the Tabernacle, this seat of worship was to be constructed according to God's specifications. Exodus Chapter 26 describes God's specifications for its construction. The outer court of the Tabernacle was to be the place where animal sacrifices were made to cover individual sins. Please note that God *never* instructed, allowed, or condoned human sacrifices in any way. Inside the Outer Court was a place called the Holy Place. This is where the High Priest was to use the Urim and Thummim (whatever they were!) to communicate with God. Inside the Holy Place was a place called the Holy of Holies, or Most Holy Place, where the High Priest was to make an atonement for the sins of Israel once a year on Yom Kippur (the Day of Atonement). This Holy of Holies was continually covered by a veil to separate it from the rest of the Tabernacle. It is also the place where the Shekinah Glory Cloud and the Ark of the Covenant resided.

The Ark of the Covenant

God instructed the Israelites to construct a rectangular box with loopholes and handles in it to carry into battle. The frame was made of wood and covered, inside and out, by layers of gold. It could be carried by Levites only; extreme penalties (such as immediate death) were visited upon those who disobeyed this rule. For some unknown, scientific reason, this Ark of the Covenant seemed to be imbued with strange and powerful forces. The movie, Raiders of the Lost Ark, could be more truthful than any normal, thinking person could imagine - especially at the end when the Ark is opened. Scientists and engineers have pored over the Ark's design and construction and concluded that it is a highly energized capacitor. Whatever the natural source of its power may be, God knew the correct formulae for giving it its power. The Bible is replete with stories of the Ark's power.

The cover of the Ark was adorned with two cherubim (angels) facing each other, and it was given the name of the Mercy Seat. It occupied the Holy of Holies unless God allowed it to be used for battles. In the Holy of Holies once a year on the Day of Atonement, the High Priest would sprinkle a sacrificed bull's blood on the Mercy Seat for the sins of the people.

Inside the Ark, Moses was instructed to put the tablets of the Ten Commandments, a pot of manna, the original scrolls of the first five books of the Bible (the Pentateuch or, for Jews, the Torah), and Aaron's budded rod (which was the only rod of many to bud in order to substantiate Aaron as Israel's High Priest). The Mercy Seat of the Ark was the only thing that prevented the cherubim on the Mercy Seat from seeing the contents of the Ark. When the Mercy Seat was sprinkled with blood, the cherubim (symbolically) could no longer see the contents of the Ark which, in turn, represented man's rebellions against God. That the bull's blood was a symbol of the future Messiah's blood shed to cover the sins of the world is immediately apparent.

The Ark was either carried off by the Babylonians or hidden during the siege of Jerusalem. Its whereabouts, today, is not known; many interesting books, tapes, and movies have addressed its possible location. Some believe it is under the Temple Mount; some believe it is on Mt. Nebo; some believe it is in Ethiopia; etc.

The Temple

The Temple was to be a permanent substitution for the Tabernacle. It was basically the same thing. The Jews, today, are more concerned over the Temple than any other religious construction. The first Temple was constructed by King Solomon around 1000 B.C. The second Temple was constructed when the Jews returned to their homeland and was embellished by King Herod of New Testament fame. This Temple was destroyed by the Romans in 70 A.D. The Jews, today, are looking for the construction of a third Temple today on its original foundations.

The Judges

At first, God ran His Israeli Theocracy through judges. No, these judges were not the kind of legal judges that one finds seated on a court bench today. These judges were called by God to deliver Israel out of the hands of her enemies. Israel, at first, was a loose-knit conglomeration of tribes scattered all across the land. When Israel became disobedient to God, He would no longer protect them from their enemies. Without God's protection, the loose-knit conglomeration was easily subdued by its enemies.

Enemies would usually require tribute from the tribes or enslave their inhabitants. The suffering imposed by the conquerors would cause Israel to cry out to God for deliverance. To relieve their agony, God would call out some kind of charismatic or military leader to deliver them. Their call was always a temporary one. The leaders, called by God to deliver the Jews, were called the judges.

Unfortunately, this cycle would repeat over and over. Each time, Israeli disobedience would become mired into deeper depravity. Eventually they no longer recognized God as their king. God, obviously, could see where this was leading. This forced Him to lament, several times in the Book of Judges:

> In those days there was no king in Israel: every man did that which was right in his own eyes. (Judg 21:25)

Force that phrase into your psyche: "every man did that which was right in his own eyes."! Once again a kind, loving, and beneficent God was rejected. This is the rebellious nature of all of mankind; even when our conscience convicts us of wrongdoing, we determine to do things our own way - regardless of the consequences. As Augustine once stated, there is, within each and every one of us, a God-shaped vacuum that God purposely Created in us. We can never be truly satisfied or happy without filling that vacuum with God.

The Kings

God had purposely gone out of His way to keep the Israelites happy: He had performed many miraculous acts on their behalf; He had them make the Ark of the Covenant to frighten their enemies and atone for their sins; He delivered them from their punishments when they were disobedient (whether from their enemies or from plagues or natural disasters); He appeared to them perpetually in the shape of the Shekinah Glory Cloud over the Holy of Holies in the Tabernacle; He had His high priests construct the Urim and Thummim (a group of precious stones on the high priests' garments. No one is really sure what these really were; it's only described in the Bible this way.) to communicate directly with Him, etc. In short, God did every thing He could think of to insure the Jews happiness and security. Unfortunately, all this wasn't, apparently, enough. Because, under their judge Samuel, the Jews demanded a human king:

> And it came to pass, when Samuel was old, that he made his sons judges over Israel. Now the name of his firstborn was Joel; and the name of his second, Abiah: they were judges in Beersheba. And his sons walked not in his ways, but turned aside after lucre, and took bribes, and perverted judgment. Then all the elders of Israel gathered themselves together, and came to Samuel unto Ramah, And said unto him, Behold, thou art old, and thy sons walk not in thy ways: now make us a king to judge us like all the nations. But the thing displeased Samuel, when they said, Give us a king to judge us. And Samuel prayed unto the LORD. And the LORD said unto Samuel, Hearken unto the voice of the people in all that they say unto thee: for they have not rejected thee, but they have rejected me, that I should not reign over them. According to all the works which they have done since the day that I brought them up out of Egypt even unto this day, wherewith they have forsaken me, and served other gods, so do they also unto thee. Now therefore hearken unto their voice: howbeit yet protest solemnly unto them, and shew them the manner of the king that shall reign over them. And Samuel told all the words of the LORD unto the people that asked of him a king. And he said, This will be the manner of the king that shall reign over you: He will take your sons, and appoint them for himself, for his chariots, and to be his horsemen; and some shall run before his chariots. And he will appoint him captains over thousands, and captains over fifties; and will set them to ear his ground, and to reap his harvest, and to make his instruments of war, and

> instruments of his chariots. And he will take your daughters to be confectionaries, and to be cooks, and to be bakers. And he will take your fields, and your vineyards, and your oliveyards, even the best of them, and give them to his servants. And he will take the tenth of your seed, and of your vineyards, and give to his officers, and to his servants. And he will take your menservants, and your maidservants, and your goodliest young men, and your asses, and put them to his work. He will take the tenth of your sheep: and ye shall be his servants. And ye shall cry out in that day because of your king which ye shall have chosen you; and the LORD will not hear you in that day. Nevertheless the people refused to obey the voice of Samuel; and they said, Nay; but we will have a king over us; That we also may be like all the nations; and that our king may judge us, and go out before us, and fight our battles. And Samuel heard all the words of the people, and he rehearsed them in the ears of the LORD. And the LORD said to Samuel, Hearken unto their voice, and make them a king. And Samuel said unto the men of Israel, Go ye every man unto his city. (1 Sam 8:1-22)

We have repeated the entirety of I Samuel Chapter 8 in order to show the entire context of Israel's demand for a human king! Apparently, Samuel's sons were ungodly men. Since Samuel was the last judge of Israel, it was obviously taken, by the Jews, that Samuel's sons would be appointed by God as the next judges over Israel. This, however, was a ruse because God did not favor men because of their stations or importance but only for their godliness. Samuel, at first, thought that Israel was rejecting him; but God reassured Samuel that they weren't rejecting Samuel but God. God, through Samuel, attempted to warn them that a human king would require taxes of them, conscript their sons and daughters into his service, confiscate their land, etc. But they still insisted because, as God told Samuel, they had rejected God's reign over them by serving after other gods (demons?).

God gave them what they wanted (I Sam 9). He selected a man from the tribe of Benjamin who was head and shoulders taller than the rest of them, was strong, intelligent, and apparently godly. This man, Israel's first king, was Saul of the tribe of Benjamin. Eventually Saul would prove unstable and disobedient to God and, as God had promised them, would require the very things of the Jews that God had warned them about.

Why was Saul chosen from the tribe of Benjamin when the tribe of Judah (Gen 49:10) was promised the kingly inheritance?

> **And it came to pass about three months after, that it was told Judah, saying, Tamar thy daughter in law hath played the harlot; and also, behold, she is with child by whoredom. And Judah said, Bring her forth, and let her be burnt. When she was brought forth, she sent to her father in law, saying, By the man, whose these are, am I with child: and she said, Discern, I pray thee, whose are these, the signet, and bracelets, and staff. And Judah acknowledged them, and said, She hath been more righteous than I; because that I gave her not to Shelah my son. And he knew her again no more. (Gen 38:24-26)**

This story, from the Book of Genesis, tells the story of Judah's incestuous relationship with his daughter-in-law, Tamar. What had happened was that Tamar was originally married to Judah's oldest son, Er. When God required the life of Er because of his ungodliness, Judah commanded that Tamar be wed to his next oldest son in accordance with the Law. The same thing happened to Judah's next oldest son. Judah then lied about his youngest son's age in order to keep him from marrying Tamar and have the same fate befall him. When Judah's wife had died, Judah went on a trip to sell his sheep. Here he encountered Tamar disguised as a prostitute. After sleeping with her, the only payment she would accept was Judah's signet, bracelets, and staff. These identified

Judah and later saved Tamar's life when she showed them to Judah. Notice the end of the story: Judah felt guilty for the unjust way he treated Tamar by not giving her his youngest son to wed. Please read the whole story: all of Genesis 38. Later when God gave His commandments to the Jews, He Commanded:

> A bastard shall not enter into the congregation of the LORD; even to his tenth generation shall he not enter into the congregation of the LORD. (Deut 23:2)

Pharez, one of Tamar's twins through this union with Judah, was the one through whom Judah's kingly promises would be realized. He was a bastard! When the Jews demanded a king from the Lord, the tenth generation from Pharez was not yet complete! Count them:

> And Tamar his daughter in law bare him Pharez and Zerah. All the sons of Judah were five. The sons of Pharez; Hezron, and Hamul. And the sons of Zerah; Zimri, and Ethan, and Heman, and Calcol, and Dara: five of them in all. And the sons of Carmi; Achar, the troubler of Israel, who transgressed in the thing accursed. And the sons of Ethan; Azariah. The sons also of Hezron, that were born unto him; Jerahmeel, and Ram, and Chelubai. And Ram begat Amminadab; and Amminadab begat Nahshon, prince of the children of Judah; And Nahshon begat Salma, and Salma begat Boaz, And Boaz begat Obed, and Obed begat Jesse, And Jesse begat his firstborn Eliab, and Abinadab the second, and Shimma the third, Nethaneel the fourth, Raddai the fifth, Ozem the sixth, David the seventh: (1 Chr 2:4-15)

We have Judah (1), Pharez (2), Hezron (3), Ram (4), Amminadab (5), Nahshon (6), Salma, (7), Boaz (8), Obed (9), Jesse (10), and David (11). Is not the consistency of God amazing?

During Saul's reign, he became more and more unstable and disobedient to God. Eventually when the tenth generation from

Pharez had run its course, David, the son of Jesse (the tenth generation from Pharez), was anointed as the new king of Israel. Unfortunately, Saul was still the king! When Saul learned of Samuel's anointing of David, he pursued David throughout the land of Palestine until his death. Interestingly of Saul's family inheritance to the throne, only a crippled, maladjusted child remained whom David took into his house and treated with kindness.

Because God loved the faithful David, He promised that the Messiah would come through his lineage:

> **Ought ye not to know that the LORD God of Israel gave the kingdom over Israel to David for ever, even to him and to his sons by a covenant of salt? (2 Chr 13:5)**
>
> **Howbeit the LORD would not destroy the house of David, because of the covenant that he had made with David, and as he promised to give a light to him and to his sons for ever. (2 Chr 21:7)**

This promise is known as the Davidic Covenant, and it is, obviously, unconditional.

David's son Solomon reigned over Israel after David. During Solomon's reign, the Temple was constructed. This was, instead of the temporary and movable Tabernacle, the permanent House of God. After Solomon's reign, the elders of Israel argued about the heavy burden of taxes imposed upon them by Solomon. Rehoboam, Solomon's son, basically told the elders that Solomon's tax burdens would be light considering what he would require. This caused a schism. Ten of the tribes split from the tribes of Judah and Benjamin and located in the northern parts of Palestine. They called themselves Israel, appointed Jeroboam as their king, and set up idol worship, to replace Temple worship, in the cities of Bethel and Dan (I Kings 12:26-29). The two tribes of Judah (from which the word Jew is derived) and Benjamin called themselves collectively Judah (after the largest tribe) and kept their capital at Jerusalem where Temple worship continued.

It is interesting to note that during their histories, which can be read in I Kings, II Kings, I Chronicles, and II Chronicles, that Israel and Judah both had 19 kings to reign over each. Israel's kings were:

-1. Jeroboam, twenty-two years

-2. Nadab, about two years

-3. Baasha, twenty-four years

-4. Elah, two years

-5. Zimri, seven days

-6. Omri, twelve years

-7. Ahab, twenty-two years

-8. Ahaziah, two years

-9. Jehoram, twelve years

-10. Jehu, twenty-eight years

-11. Jehoahaz, seventeen years

-12. Jehoash, sixteen years

-13. Jeroboam II, forty-one years

-14. Zachariah, six months

-15. Shallum, one month

-16. Menahem, ten years

-17. Pekahiah, two years

-18. Pekah, twenty years

-19. Hoshea, nine years

All 19 of Israel's kings were ungodly. Judah's kings were:

-1. Rehoboam, seventeen years

-2. Abijah (Abijam), three years

-3. Asa, forty-one years

-4. Jehoshaphat, twenty-five years

-5. Jehoram, eight years

-6. Ahaziah, one year

-7. Joash (Jehoash), forty years

-8. Amaziah, twenty-nine years

-9. Uzziah (Azariah), fifty-two years

-10. Jotham, sixteen years

-11. Ahaz, sixteen years

-12. Hezekiah, twenty-nine years

-13. Manasseh, fifty-five years

-14. Amon, two years

-15. Josiah, thirty-one years

-16. Jehoahaz (Josiah's son), three months

-17. Jehoiakim (Josiah's son), eleven years

-18. Jehoiachin (Jeconiah), Jehoiakim's son, three months

-19. Zedekiah (Mattaniah), Josiah's son, eleven years

About half of Judah's king were ungodly; the rest were godly. One of the more interesting godly kings of Judah was their 12th king, Hezekiah. I highly recommend further reading about him through commentaries or other literature.

Because the Jews of both kingdoms were continually disobedient to God, God finally punished them by sending them off into captivity. Israel was sent to Assyria in 722 B.C., and Judah was sent to Babylon in 597 B.C. During the Babylonian siege of Jerusalem, the Temple was sacked. Babylon, in turn, was conquered by the Persians. Eventually, the Jews in Babylon under Persian rule, were, under Nehemiah, allowed to return to Palestine, restore their land, and repopulate their land. A new Temple was constructed.

The Jews, returning from captivity, learned one thing never to be repeated: not to worship idols. Before their captivity, idolatry was practiced in the Temple (God's house) itself. In fact, the

Bible actually records the practice of the Jews in worshipping the Queen of Heaven (i.e., Semiramis whom we have already discussed) and weeping for her son Tammuz (whom we've also discussed) by name.

> **Then he brought me to the door of the gate of the LORD's house which was toward the north; and, behold, there sat women weeping for Tammuz. (Ezek 8:14)**

Why were the women weeping for Tammuz? Depending on which legend is taken, Tammuz was supposedly out hunting when he was killed by a wild boar. For 40 days he lay dead until, miraculously, he was resurrected. Sound familiar? This is where we get our modern notions of Lent and Easter from. The queen of heaven is mentioned five times in the Bible (Jer 7:18; Jer 44:17-19,25).

The 400-some odd years following the Jews return to the land are called the silent years because God discontinued sending prophets to them. The next great prophet to arise in the land of Judea was John the Baptist.

The Romans' sacking of the second Temple was accomplished in 70 A.D. Because the Jews were a constant antagonism to the Romans, the Romans pursued and hunted them down wherever they could be found. The Jews found refuge in lands other than their beloved Judea. This is known as the **Diaspora**. It is not totally clear where the Dispensation of Law ends: the sacking of the Temple, Jesus' resurrection, Pentecost, etc. What is clear, however, is that this dispensation ends, and the Jews are punished for killing God's only begotten Son, Jesus.

Chapter 9

DISPENSATION 6: GRACE

We could very easily have taken a lot more space to give Dispensation 5 (the Law) the justice it requires. We could have discussed the nature of the animal sacrifices, the Ten Commandments in much greater detail, a more complete and comprehensive history of the Jews, etc. Hopefully, we have covered enough material from Dispensation 5 to fully explain the necessary details of this dispensation. Other material will be introduced as the necessity arises.

Even though John the Baptist and Jesus were not present when we believe this dispensation began, we believe that their ministries were the catalysts for this dispensation - especially Jesus'. This Dispensation, and God's requirement of Grace, is covered through the entirety of the New Testament.

The Bible states emphatically, several times, that Jesus originally came to restore the lost house of Israel. The Jews knew of this man, prophetically, as the Messiah. This means that He, if accepted by the nation's leaders, would throw off the Roman oppressors and restore Israel as a Theocratic kingdom. When this failed (which He knew would happen, as God), He died as a living sacrifice for the sins of the world. Men needed no longer obey the

Law but to simply have faith in His power to save them. This is a complex subject which we shall try to treat humbly, reverently, and honestly in more depth in this chapter.

After His Resurrection and departure, the Holy Spirit visited the disciples on the day of Pentecost. Once they were imbued with this godly power, they began to preach the Gospel (Good News) of Salvation to the world. This is when we believe this dispensation began.

If we truly believe in the Dispensational Theory, we must be careful not to mix the dispensations of Law and Grace. The Dispensation of Law was given to the Jews to spread to the entire world. This, they failed to do. The Dispensation of Grace was given to all mankind (including the Jews). Just because God has set up a new testament with mankind does not mean that He has forgotten His original, unconditional covenant with the Jews. This covenant was made to the literal descendants of Abraham, Isaac, Jacob, and the 12 sons of Jacob. Christians who believe that God has replaced His promise to the Jews and now intends it for the Christians are kidding themselves. How much plainer could God's language be? Do the Christians who believe that God's original promises to the Jews also incorporate God's curses to them? How many Gentiles are descended from Abraham? None!

Jesus

If we recall the Protevangelium, the Messiah would be the "seed of the woman". That this implied a virgin conception is explained more fully by the prophecy of Isaiah 7:14 which we have already discussed. In the ancient literature, the Jews, in their rabbinic literature, and the Muslims, in the Koran, referred to Jesus as "the son of Mary". No father's name was ever attached to Jesus. The fact that Jesus' biological father could never be identified by the ancients implies a literal, and historic, fulfillment of the biblical prophecies.

That honor and reverence should be accorded to Mary as the chosen mother of Jesus is obvious. Worship and sublimation to the status of "queen of heaven", however, is definitely contradictory to the Ten Commandments ("Thou shalt have no other gods before thee").

When Mary was pregnant with Jesus, the angel, Gabriel, instructed her to name the child "Jesus". This is the Greek equivalent to the Hebrew name "Joshua". It is an instructive name because it literally means "God (i.e., Yahweh, the name of God) is salvation". In Hebrew, His name was literally Yeshua, which means "salvation". Could God have been any clearer as to Jesus' divine identity? Furthermore, He was called "the Christ". This is the Greek equivalent of the Hebrew word "Messiah". Messiah literally means "the anointed one". This, then, is not a name but a title. It is also instructive. Hebrew kings were anointed with special oil. Thus, the Jews expected a king. They did not anticipate just any king, but they expected a special king, called the Messiah, appointed by God. The Jews, however, could not clearly reconcile the prophecies that called for the Messiah to be a suffering king and, at the same time, a conquering hero. They reasoned, therefore, in one coming of two Messiahs instead of two comings of one Messiah. We've already covered the two-Messiah concept previously which explains one of the many reasons the Jews rejected Jesus as their Messiah.

The fact that Jesus' life as a youngster is seldom mentioned in the Bible is a fact that we should respect. We know that Jesus was sinless even during those years. He had to be! How could anyone die as a substitute sacrifice for the sins of the world if He had His own sin debt to pay? The only way that Jesus could be a substitute, sinless sacrifice and fulfill the prophecy of the Protevangelium was as God. The only way He could inherit rule over the entire earth was as a man. God, foreseeing this 4,000 years before, accomplished this in Jesus. This combination of God and man in one individual is called **the hypostatic union**. He had all the powers of God and all the limitations of man. Since this combination produces all kinds of contradictory ramifications to our finite minds, this must remain a Christian mystery. Faith is definitely required here. Suffice it to say that He was as much God as if He had never been a man and as much a man as if He had never been God.

An excellent purpose of the hypostatic union can be demonstrated.

> **For there is one God, and one mediator between God and men, the man Christ Jesus; (1 Tim 2:5)**

Advocacy is the proper duty of a priest. Thus, Jesus is our high priest. We are to confess our sins to Him alone. No man, whether he be a Catholic priest or any other man, deserves to hear our sins. All men are sinners, and they have their own imperfections to answer for. But another result of Jesus' God-man status can be summed up in this verse. Jesus, as a sinless man, knows us and our complete impotence to obey God. When we confess our sins to the *man* Jesus, He can immediately forgive us as the *God* Jesus! Once again, the perfection and completion of God's Plan is demonstrated.

The Bible, especially the Gospels (Matthew, Mark, Luke, and John), begin Jesus' life with His mission to the Jews at about the age of thirty (Luke 3:23). This mission began with the singular act of Jesus' baptism in the Jordan River. At this point, the Holy Spirit, in the form of a dove, descended upon Jesus. Also at this point, Jesus no longer used His powers as God; instead He used the power endowed upon Him by the Holy Spirit. Of course, you're going to say that it is not only hard to believe that Jesus performed all of His recorded miracles in the Holy Spirit's power but if He had the power to begin with He should never have relinquished it to another person of the Godhead. Believe it or not, He did this as an instruction to us! By His life as an example, He showed us how we, too, could overcome the power of sin in our lives and, in obedience, perform miracles!

> **Let this mind be in you, which was also in Christ Jesus: Who, being in the form of God, thought it not robbery to be equal with God: But made himself of no reputation, and took upon him the form of a servant, and was made in the likeness of men: And being found in fashion as a man, he humbled himself,**

> **and became obedient unto death, even the death of the cross. (Phil 2:5-8)**

The King James version translates the Greek word "kenoo" as "of no reputation". This translation, however, is not quite literally correct. Strong's Hebrew/Greek Concordance defines it thusly:

> 2758 kenoo (ken-o'-o); from 2756; to make empty, i.e. (figuratively) to abase, neutralize, falsify: KJV-- make (of none effect, of no reputation, void), be in vain.

Instead of "but made himself of no reputation" the verse should read "but emptied himself". Because of the Greek word, this doctrine is known as **the kenosis of Christ**. In an act of *absolute humility*, He denied Himself in obedience to the Father. That is, He emptied Himself of His own Godly power!

How can the kenosis of Christ be instructive to us? God, remember, knows all things. Therefore, He knows us. He also knows that we have no power or compulsion to obey His Will. Oh, we may wish to, but we can't! When we are saved (i.e., trust in Jesus' power over death to save us), we are immediately given the present of the indwelling Holy Spirit:

> **In whom ye also trusted, after that ye heard the word of truth, the gospel of your salvation: in whom also after that ye believed, ye were sealed with that holy Spirit of promise, Which is the earnest of our inheritance until the redemption of the purchased possession, unto the praise of his glory. (Eph 1:13-14)**

Notice that this passage says that we are *sealed* with the Holy Spirit! All Christians receive Him. This is known as the **baptism in the Holy Spirit**. How, then, can we use the Holy Spirit to overcome sin in our lives? Believe it or not, it is so simple it is almost embarrassing. The answer is *prayer.* Other passages in the Scriptures tell us that, because we're human, we will eventually sin again even if we're filled with the Holy Spirit. To restore the Holy Spirit's power over our lives, we must come to God humbly, ask Him to forgive our sins, and to refill us with the Holy Spirit.

Why should He accede to our prayers? Because He promised!!! God, remember, never lies! Thus, it is possible to be baptized in the Holy Spirit many times in our lives. Each time we're baptized, the Holy Spirit fills us and takes control over us as we submit our wills to His. We, however, are a peculiarly rebellious and independent breed. We like to control our own wills! Therefore, we find ourselves almost continuously without the Holy Spirit's control over our lives; very often, we must ask for continual baptism in the Spirit many times in one day. At first, this practice will seem tedious; but the more we practice this, the more we will recognize the guiding and gentle hand of God in our lives! Is not our God not only glorious but loving, kind, complete, and omniscient? You BET He is!!!! *No* god of any other religion can come close to competing in these qualities!

> **My little children, these things write I unto you, that ye sin not. And if any man sin, we have an advocate with the Father, Jesus Christ the righteous: And he is the propitiation for our sins: and not for ours only, but also for the sins of the whole world. (I Jn 2:1-2)**

There are many wonderful texts that refer to these Christian doctrines and more.

End of the Christian Age

Since we believe that we are currently in the sixth millennium, the Age of Grace, this age has not yet ended. In order to understand how this age will end, we must consult prophecy. Fortunately, the Bible says much about this.

God must still fulfill His ancient promises to Abraham and his offspring (i.e., the Jews). Otherwise, He would be proven to be either a liar or another of those other impotent religious gods. Right now, however, He is continuing to deal with Jew and Gentile alike in His Church. This must be ended and attention once more focused on the Jews. How God ends His dealings with the Church, during this Age, is fascinatingly portrayed in Scripture. God will snatch all Christians from the earth in one mighty act transforming their mortal bodies into immortal ones with a whole generation of Christians never experiencing death! Remember the italicized portion of the quote from The Decline and Fall of the Roman Empire? This is what we're explaining now. It is also the removal of fundamentalist Christians from the earth who would otherwise oppose a new world order as explained by the New Age Movement discussed earlier. This act is called **the rapture** by Christians and literally means a snatching away. To prove this assertion biblically, we quote:

> Behold, I shew you a mystery; We shall not all sleep, but we shall all be changed, In a moment, in the twinkling of an eye, at the last trump: for the trumpet shall sound, and the dead shall be raised incorruptible, and we shall be changed. For this corruptible must put on incorruption, and this mortal must put on immortality. So when this corruptible shall have put on incorruption, and this mortal shall have put on immortality, then shall be brought to pass the saying that is written, Death is swallowed up in victory. O death, where is thy sting? O grave, where is thy victory? The sting of death is sin; and the strength of sin is the law. But thanks be to God, which giveth us the victory through our Lord Jesus Christ. Therefore, my beloved brethren, be ye stedfast, unmoveable, always abounding in the work of the Lord, forasmuch as ye know that your labour is not in vain in the Lord. (1 Cor 15:51-58)

Another passage:

> But I would not have you to be ignorant, brethren, concerning them which are asleep, that ye sorrow not, even as others which have no hope. For if we believe that Jesus died and rose again, even so them also which sleep in Jesus will God bring with him. For this we say unto you by the word of the Lord, that we which are alive and remain unto the coming of

> the Lord shall not prevent them which are asleep. For the Lord himself shall descend from heaven with a shout, with the voice of the archangel, and with the trump of God: and the dead in Christ shall rise first: Then we which are alive and remain shall be caught up together with them in the clouds, to meet the Lord in the air: and so shall we ever be with the Lord. Wherefore comfort one another with these words. (1Thes 4:13-18)

That these two, separate passages relate to the same event is unquestionable. The event will be signaled by the "last trumpet". The "last trumpet" is pregnant with meaning but, for now, simply means the blowing of a trumpet. To find out more about this "last trumpet", I highly recommend Joseph Good's book, Rosh Hashanah and the Messianic Kingdom to Come. Both passages relate to the resurrection of the dead. Then phrases such as "we shall be changed", "this mortal must put on immortality", "O grave, where is thy victory?", and "Then we which are alive and remain shall be caught up" tells us that an entire generation of living Christians will not experience death! With this event out of the way (the Rapture), God can turn His attention to fulfilling His promises to the Jews.

Once the Christians are gone, the next age can commence. The age will end in the worst period of Judgment in the history of the world called "The Tribulation". The next age is called, in the Bible, "the Day of the Lord".

The doctrine of a "pre-tribulation rapture" is, unfortunately, a hotly disputed topic for evangelical Christians. There are other views such as a mid-tribulation rapture, a post-tribulation rapture, and a post-millennium rapture. We will discuss, at some length, the biblical doctrine of the tribulation in the next chapter. This is a period of time (seven years) when the earth will go through the worst testing in all its history. The millennium (which will also be discussed in the next chapter) is the seventh age of Jesus' reign on earth for one thousand years. The mid-tribulation rapture argument stems from the idea that God's wrath will not be released on the earth until halfway through the tribulation, and God will only exempt His Christians from His wrath. The post-tribulation rapture and post-millennium rapture is based on an obviously discarded notion from Scripture interpreted figuratively. That is, adherents to these views maintain that mankind is continually "evolving" spiritually, and, when Jesus returns, the Church will be the sole religion of the entire earth and will hand over its rule to Him.

We hold to a pre-tribulation rapture for many reasons. For one, the end of the Church Age will be clearly marked. Once God no longer has a reason to protect His Church, He can turn His attention to the Jews exclusively. For another, the plain words of Scripture teach such a notion.

> Now we beseech you, brethren, by the coming of our Lord Jesus Christ, and *by* our gathering together unto him, That ye be not soon shaken in mind, or be troubled, neither by spirit, nor by word, nor by letter as from us, as that the day of Christ is at hand. Let no man deceive you by any means: for *that day shall not come,* except there come a falling away first, and that man of sin be revealed, the son of perdition; Who opposeth and exalteth himself above all that is called God, or that is worshipped; so that he as God sitteth in the temple of God, shewing himself that he is God. (2Thess. 2:1-4)

The Greek word translated as "a falling away" is "apostasia" and should be translated as "a catching away". According to Kenneth Wuest, a renowned Greek scholar, this "catching away" is a *physical* catching away. In other words, the rapture! This Greek word, apostasia, is only used twice in the entire Bible. Doctor Wuest, however, has come across this word in other Greek works such as Homer's Iliad. It means a retreat. That is, it is a military word that means to physically fall back. The other usage (Acts 21:21) is translated as "forsake" when discussing the Gentiles treatment of following the law of Moses. In this case, a defection is probably the correct translation. But when it comes to our "gathering together unto him", the physical movement makes more sense. With all of the secularism taking root in today's society, how could we possibly measure how severe a "falling away" would be to signal the return of our Lord? Remember, there will still be Christians on the earth at the Rapture. They must be taken in order to allow Satan's rule to begin.

To translate this correctly, we would have the following:

> Now we beseech you, brethren, by the coming of our Lord Jesus Christ, and by our gathering together unto him, That ye be not soon shaken in mind, or be troubled, neither by spirit, nor by word, nor by letter as from us, as that the tribulation is at hand. Let no man deceive you by any means: for that day shall not come, except there come the rapture first, and that man of sin be revealed, the son of perdition.....

If this translation doesn't support a pre-tribulation rapture, I don't know what other argument I could make to make it any plainer.

The phrase "the day of Christ" is also a slight mistranslation and should be translated as "the day of the Lord" – or, the tribulation.

> Blow ye the trumpet in Zion, and sound an alarm in my holy mountain: let all the inhabitants of the land tremble: for the day of the LORD cometh, for *it is* nigh at hand; A day of darkness and of gloominess, a day of clouds and of thick darkness, as the morning spread upon the mountains: a great people and a strong; there hath not been ever the like, neither shall be any more after it, *even* to the years of many generations. (Joel 2:1-2)

As can be seen, the day of the Lord which is synonymous with the Millennium, is the worst time of testing in the history of the earth. Only the very first seven years of the Millennium will be this horrible time. This, according to the Mount Olivet discourse, is the same time known as the tribulation.

Therefore, evangelical Christians believe in two future comings of our Lord, Jesus: the Rapture and the Second Advent. Both of these mark important time periods in God's Plan. The Rapture ends the Age of Grace; the Second Advent ends the Tribulation. It is important that true, evangelical Christians understand the difference between these two. At the Rapture, Jesus comes secretly for His Church (i.e., in the clouds, 1 Thess. 4:17). At the Second Advent, every eye shall see Him (Rev. 1:7). At the Rapture, Jesus doesn't touch down to earth (1 Thess. 4:17). At the Second Advent, Jesus comes to the earth at the Mount of Olives (Zech. 14:4). At the Rapture, Jesus comes to reward His saints (1 Thess. 5:9-11). At the Second Coming, Jesus comes to punish all those who have rejected Him (Rev. 19:15-21). At the Rapture, Jesus comes for His saints (1 Thess. 4:14). At the Second Coming, Jesus comes with His saints (Jude 1:14-15).

There are other contrasts, but these should suffice to point out the differences. Once again, please make doubly sure that these two events are clearly understood and remembered because, as already stated, they mark important events in the time frame of God's Plan.

Chapter 10

DISPENSATION 7: THE KINGDOM

We now discuss the last Age in God's Plan for the redemption of mankind: The Kingdom (also called the Millennium and the Sabbath Age). This age, unlike the others, will begin with the suffering of all of mankind. It will be marked by a singular, and clearly noticeable, act. To understand this, we will have to refer to ancient prophecy.

God's Prophecies to the Jews

Back in the Age of the Law, the Jews failed, as a nation, to obey God and make themselves a separated nation unto Him as a witness to the world. As a consequence, God had to punish them several times. One of the most severe punishments God exacted on the Jewish nation was to have them fall captive to the Assyrians and Babylonians and have them exiled to these nations – removing them from the land. After Solomon's death and during his son's, Rehoboam's, reign, the Jews became encumbered under the heavy tax burden exacted upon them by Solomon. Rather than listen to the people's complaints, Rehoboam promised them an even heavier tax burden than his father, Solomon, had levied on them. Under Jereboam's leadership, ten of the tribes decided to rebel against Rehoboam and form their own kingdom. This they did, and they called their new kingdom Israel and established a new capital at Samaria. The two remaining tribes were comprised of the two tribes of Judah and Benjamin, named their kingdom after the much more populous tribe of Judah, and kept their capital at Jerusalem.

Since the Temple resided in Jerusalem, the Jewish sacrificial system went on in Jerusalem without modification. This presented problems for Jereboam because many Jews from Israel continually traveled to the Temple in Jerusalem to observe the Jewish rituals. In response, he set up an idolatrous system of worship in Samaria to keep his people at home. Unfortunately, this kept most of the Levites, the priestly tribe who had no landed inheritance, in Jerusalem with the Temple. The Bible, henceforth, records not one king in Israel's history as a godly king. In contrast, about half of the kings of Judah are recorded as godly kings. Because of this, Israel went into captivity in Assyria almost two hundred years before Judah. Judah eventually had a series of ungodly kings, towards the end of her history, which led to her captivity in Babylon. At this time, the Temple was destroyed, and the Temple treasures were carried off to Babylon.

When the Judahites were carried off to Babylon, a certain class of intelligent, educated Jews was exiled into King Nebuchadnezzar's court to train them in the Babylonian mystery religion. Among these was the Prophet Daniel. God revealed some amazing prophecies and promises to this humble prophet. One of the prophecies God had revealed to the Prophet Jeremiah which Daniel understood was that Judah, at least, would only spend seventy years in exile in Babylon.

> In the first year of his reign I Daniel understood by books the number of the years, whereof the word of the LORD came to Jeremiah the prophet, that he would accomplish seventy years in the desolations of Jerusalem. (Dan 9:2)

> And this whole land shall be a desolation, and an astonishment; and these nations shall serve the king of Babylon seventy years. (Jer 25:11)

> For thus saith the LORD, That after seventy years be accomplished at Babylon I will visit you, and perform my good word toward you, in causing you to return to this place. (Jer 29:10)

Why was seventy years so significant?

> But in the seventh year shall be a sabbath of rest unto the land, a sabbath for the LORD: thou shalt neither sow thy field, nor prune thy vineyard. (Lev 25:4)

As we can see, the Jews were required to leave their land fallow every seventh year as a Sabbath to the Lord. They had not done this for 490 years! Every seventh year of 490 years is the 70 years that the Jews owed God. So while the Jews were in captivity for 70 years, the land remained fallow as God commanded!

While Daniel was contemplating this, he realized that the long season of captivity was almost accomplished (he was an old man by this time). He prayed to the Lord to forgive Judah's sins. Notice that even though Daniel, himself, was not guilty of these sins, he included himself, in complete humility, as one of those who had sinned. In response to his prayer and humility, God sent the archangel Gabriel to him. We have previously quoted these verses.

Starting in verse 24 ("Seventy weeks..."), Gabriel announces to Daniel that God has set a definite time frame for the Jewish people. Weeks, in ancient Hebrew, is literally "sevens". These sevens could be hours, days, weeks, months, or years. Because Daniel was reading from Jeremiah's prophecy of seventy *years*, most biblical scholars understand these sevens to be years. If this is true, then the Jews would once again become a prominent people in 70 * 7 = 490 years. In fact, the end of the sentence says "to anoint the most Holy". This is understood to mean the Jewish Messiah, or Jesus, the Christ. The word "anoint" means to literally crown Him as King. We know, however, that this never happened!

To understand why this has not as yet occurred, we must understand the rest of the prophecy. In the next verse, Gabriel mentions a commandment that will allow the Jews to rebuild the walls of Jerusalem. This will start the 490-year countdown. Was such a command ever issued? Yes!!! The King of Persia, who succeeded the King of Babylon, issued such a proclamation. This parchment has been uncovered archaeologically! It's been dated to March 14, 445 B.C. We must once more visit the argument mentioned previously by Sir Robert Anderson, in his excellent book The Coming Prince. He goes into the details of dating this parchment. To countdown the time from this date, we must use God's (i.e., the Jews') calendar. This calendar is a lunar calendar (unlike our present solar calendar of 365 days) and is marked by 12 months of 30 days each. Thus, the Jewish calendar is 360 days long. Making allowances for the differences between our present solar calendar of 365 days and the Jewish 360-day lunar calendar and leap years, Sir Robert Anderson was able to make some interesting and far-reaching conclusions. Please notice that the prophecy goes on to say that after the proclamation is made, the Messiah would come after seven weeks and threescore and two weeks or 69 weeks * 7 = 483 years.

Let's calculate this, as Anderson does. We have 7 x 69 = 483 years. Then we have 483 x 360 = 173,880 days. Dividing this by 365 gives us 476.38 years. In 476 years, there will be 476/4 = 119 leap years. Every year divisible by 100 is not a leap year, but years exactly divisible by 400 are. There are 3 of these years divisible by 100 in 476 years bringing our total to 116 days. The remainder of .38 years, when multiplied by 365, is 140 days. We must subtract the 116 leap year days from this total of 140 because leap year days actually increase the overall total. This gives us 476 years and 24 days. When subtracting the 445 date from 476 we must keep in mind that there was no year 0; we went from 1 B.C. to 1 A.D. Thus, we must add a year to give us 476 – 445 + 1 = 32. Thus, Jesus offered Himself as Messiah to the Jews in 32 A.D. Furthermore, adding the 24 days to March 14 inclusively (March 31 – March 14

+1 = 17 + 1 = 18 days) + the remaining 6 days from the original 24 yields the date of April 6! Anderson concludes that Jesus offered Himself as the Jewish Messiah on the very *day* prophesied in the Book of Daniel! What's even more astounding is that the Jews had no such problems with their calendar as we have with ours; they begin their calendar with Creation and count continually from there. They should have been very familiar with the 70 sevens of Daniel. Therefore, they should have immediately recognized Jesus as their Messiah on the very day predicted!

The next sentence says that after these 69 weeks (the seven weeks in the previous sentence being understood), Messiah would be cut off. This literally means that He would die! The last sentence makes reference to someone who would make a covenant with the Jews for the last week, but that in the midst of that last week he would break his promise. This is a reference to the man the early Christians called the Antichrist. So the middle of the week is of prime importance! How long did Jesus' ministry last? It lasted for 3½ years! How do we know? Jesus, according to Luke, began His ministry at about the age of 30. Counting the number of Jewish feasts that occurred in the Gospels gives us an estimate of 3½ years for Jesus' ministry! Once again, Anderson claims that April 6, 32 A.D. is the date recorded in the Gospels that we call Palm Sunday! Is there evidence for this in the Bible? You bet there is!

> O Jerusalem, Jerusalem, thou that killest the prophets, and stonest them which are sent unto thee, how often would I have gathered thy children together, even as a hen gathereth her chickens under her wings, and ye would not! Behold, your house is left unto you desolate. For I say unto you, Ye shall not see me henceforth, till ye shall say, Blessed is he that cometh in the name of the Lord. (Matt 23:37-39)

This is recorded in the Gospel of Matthew. It's what Jesus said right after He offered Himself as the Jewish King. The phrase "your house is left unto you desolate.", means that the House of David, the Jewish palace, will not be filled at this time. Need more convincing? Okay!

> And when he was come near, he beheld the city, and wept over it, Saying, If thou hadst known, even thou, at least in this thy day, the things which belong unto thy peace! but now they are hid from thine eyes. For the days shall come upon thee, that thine enemies shall cast a trench about thee, and compass thee round, and keep thee in on every side, And shall lay thee even with the ground, and thy children within thee; and they shall not leave in thee one stone upon another; because thou knewest not the time of thy visitation. (Luke 19:41-44)

Notice Jesus' words carefully. His reference to "in this thy day" meant that He spoke of a single day! His concluding remarks which end with the phrase "because thou knewest not the time of thy visitation." speaks of a certain time that the Messiah would offer Himself to the Jewish people. The prophecy beginning with the words "for the days shall come upon thee" refers to the Roman destruction of Jerusalem, and the Temple, which occurred, just as prophesied, by the Roman general Titus in 70 A.D.

That there are 3½ years left in Daniel's prophecy seems clear. But there have been approximately 2,000 years since Jesus' death. Why? If God had instituted the restoration of His Theocratic Kingdom when Jesus offered Himself, He would have gone directly from the Age of Law to the Age of the Kingdom. He would have completely bypassed the Age of Grace and, thereby, would have contradicted His original Plan of seven Ages! Not only so, but there would have been no need for Jesus' unmentionable Sacrifice on our behalf. But God knows the end from the beginning! He knew that the Hellenistic (i.e., Greek) influence on His people, the Jews, would prevent their acceptance of Jesus as their king. The priests, furthermore, were not from the priestly class of Jewish Levites that were originally ordained by God; these were political appointees. Many of the priests, at this time, had actually purchased their offices from the Romans and Herod!

So, then, why didn't the Jews of His day recognize Jesus as their Messiah? It's because the ruling priestly class of His day, the rabbis and Sanhedrin, were corruptible beyond belief. As just mentioned, most of them were either appointed to their positions by the Romans and/or Herod or had bought their offices from them. They reasoned that if the Jews recognized Jesus as their Messiah, and if they were correct, then Jesus would have immediately, and forcefully, removed the Roman authority and reinstated the Israeli state according to their own Old Testament prophecies. They further reasoned that, because they were the religious rulers of Israel who were not placed in their positions of authority according to their own, and God's, religious laws, they would lose their positions. Therefore, they had to thwart God's plan to restore Israel by deceitfully convincing the majority of the Jews that Jesus was an impostor and must be put to death. The descendents of this ruling class of rabbis continue with this deception until this very day. They have purposefully misinterpreted their own Scriptures and, even in some instances, removed some of them from their own Bibles. Paul, in the New Testament, actually prophesies about this deceit.

> **What then? Israel hath not obtained that which he seeketh for; but the election hath obtained it, and the rest were blinded (According as it is written, God hath given them the spirit of slumber, eyes that they should not see, and ears that they should not hear;) unto this day. (Rom 11:7-8)**

In other words, God allowed this deception to occur so Jesus could die for all as prophesied. This, however, does not excuse the deceit! Furthermore, ancient rabbinical commentaries on the Old Testament easily provide more than enough evidence that would clearly identify Jesus as the Messiah to the honest Jew. Remember that, in the Book of Acts, 5,000 Jews were added to the Church in a single day (Acts 4:4)! For an exhaustively documented record of this conspiracy, I recommend Philip Moore's <u>The End of History: Messiah Conspiracy</u>.

When, then, will the Jews be reinstated as God's people? For the answer to this question, we must turn to other prophecies.

The Restoration of the Jews

Before we can truly address the question of *when* God will restore His ancient people, we must first address the question of *will* God reinstate His people. After all, a popular splinter group within Christianity, called replacement theology, maintains that Christianity has *replaced* the Jews, who rejected Jesus, with Christianity. They further maintain that the Scriptures which refer to the restoration of the Jews should be interpreted symbolically and replaced by Christianity.

Way back in the Book of Genesis, we find this promise made by God to Abraham.

> **In the same day the LORD made a covenant with Abram, saying, Unto thy seed have I given this land, from the river of Egypt unto the great river, the river Euphrates: The Kenites, and the Kenizzites, and the Kadmonites, And the Hittites, and the Perizzites, and the Rephaims, And the Amorites, and the Canaanites, and the Girgashites, and the Jebusites. (Gen 15:18-21)**

The seed (i.e., the offspring of Abram) was the Jews. Abram, at this point, was not yet saved and given the name of Abraham until later. The river of Egypt has been variously identified by biblical scholars as a river that once flowed from the Mediterranean, east of the Nile, to the Red Sea separating Egypt from the Sinai peninsula. The river Euphrates is, today, within the borders of modern day Iraq! The Jews have never owned and occupied this territory throughout their history. This promise of God is an unconditional promise! If God does not keep this promise, He, then, is a liar! Thus, the fulfillment of this promise must occur some time in the future. This will occur when He restores the Jews.

To demonstrate that God will never forsake the Jews, we quote from the New Testament.

> I say then, Hath God cast away his people? God forbid. For I also am an Israelite, of the seed of Abraham, of the tribe of Benjamin. God hath not cast away his people which he foreknew. Wot ye not what the scripture saith of Elias? how he maketh intercession to God against Israel, saying, Lord, they have killed thy prophets, and digged down thine altars; and I am left alone, and they seek my life. But what saith the answer of God unto him? I have reserved to myself seven thousand men, who have not bowed the knee to the image of Baal. Even so then at this present time also there is a remnant according to the election of grace. (Rom 11:1-5)

Paul, here, is speaking of the Israelites (i.e., the Jews). Remember, the gifts and callings of God are without repentance.

We can now return to our original question of when God will restore the Jewish nation.

> Come, and let us return unto the LORD: for he hath torn, and he will heal us; he hath smitten, and he will bind us up. After two days will he revive us: in the third day he will raise us up, and we shall live in his sight. (Hosea 6:1-2)

Since this quotation comes from the Old Testament, it is a Jewish prophecy. Notice that the Jews will be punished (according to this passage) for two days and God will turn back to them in the third. Remember the theory of Dispensationalism: each day with the Lord is as a thousand years? Thus, the Jews will be punished for two thousand years for rejecting their Messiah and be revived in the third thousand year. This means that the Age of Grace will last at least two thousand years. When Jesus was crucified, He died in the afternoon and was raised in the morning of the third day. Likewise, Jesus waited at least two days after Lazarus died and raised him on the third day. Many biblical scholars believe these events are symbolic as to when Jesus will resurrect the Jews. If they're correct, then the Age of Grace will last a little longer than 2,000 years, but no one knows for sure how much longer.

But the Jews are already in their land! Why hasn't God already raised them up?

> The hand of the LORD was upon me, and carried me out in the spirit of the LORD, and set me down in the midst of the valley which was full of bones, And caused me to pass by them round about: and, behold, there were very many in the open valley; and, lo, they were very dry. And he said unto me, Son of man, can these bones live? And I answered, O Lord GOD, thou knowest. Again he said unto me, Prophesy upon these bones, and say unto them, O ye dry bones, hear the word of the LORD. Thus saith the Lord GOD unto these bones; Behold, I will cause breath to enter into you, and ye shall live: And I will lay sinews upon you, and will bring up flesh upon you, and cover you with skin, and put breath in you, and ye shall live; and ye shall know that I am the LORD. So I prophesied as I was commanded: and as I prophesied, there was a noise, and behold a shaking, and the bones came together, bone to his bone. And when I beheld, lo, the sinews and the flesh came up upon them, and the skin covered them above: but there was no breath in them. Then said he unto me, Prophesy unto the wind, prophesy, son of man, and say to the wind, Thus saith the Lord GOD; Come from the four winds, O breath, and breathe upon these slain, that they may live. So I prophesied as he commanded me, and the breath came into them, and they lived, and stood up upon their feet, an exceeding great army. Then he said unto me, Son of man, these bones are the whole house of Israel: behold, they say, Our bones are dried, and our hope is lost: we are cut off for our parts. Therefore prophesy and say unto

> them. Thus saith the Lord GOD; Behold, O my people, I will open your graves, and cause you to come up out of your graves, and bring you into the land of Israel. And ye shall know that I am the LORD, when I have opened your graves, O my people, and brought you up out of your graves, And shall put my spirit in you, and ye shall live, and I shall place you in your own land: then shall ye know that I the LORD have spoken it, and performed it, saith the LORD. (Ezek 37:1-14)

This famous prophecy is, admittedly, filled with symbolism. Please notice about ¾ of the way down, the prophecy explains itself! God is symbolically explaining a process that will one day eventuate into turning many of the godless Jews back to seeking Him and recognizing Jesus as their Messiah. First, He will open the graves, and bring the Jews back to Israel. Next, He will put sinews and flesh on their bones. This speaks of power. Israel is recognized, today, as the third strongest country on earth after only the United States and Russia. Finally, He will put His Spirit in them. This will only occur after they, as a nation, recognize Jesus as their Messiah. The Bible predicts, emphatically, that this will happen.

> And I will pour upon the house of David, and upon the inhabitants of Jerusalem, the spirit of grace and of supplications: and they shall look upon me whom they have pierced, and they shall mourn for him, as one mourneth for his only son, and shall be in bitterness for him, as one that is in bitterness for his firstborn. (Zech 12:10)

This will occur only after a bitter struggle that pits the world against Israel. The Jews, in utter desperation, can see that their only ally is Jesus! What an ally! Finally, they turn to Him. For an interesting perspective of this whole picture, Chapters 12 to 14 of Zechariah should be read.

Are we then in the last days before the return of Jesus? Let's allow Scripture to answer this question.

> **Now learn a parable of the fig tree; When his branch is yet tender, and putteth forth leaves, ye know that summer is nigh: So likewise ye, when ye shall see all these things, know that it is near, even at the doors. Verily I say unto you, This generation shall not pass, till all these things be fulfilled. (Matt 24:32-34)**

Throughout the Scriptures, Israel is likened to a fig tree. Between 70 A.D. and 1948 A.D., Israel was not a nation. Israel became a nation, again, in 1948. This parable of Jesus is a reference to His Second Coming. Jesus, then, seems to be saying that His Second Coming will occur within one generation after Israel is restored as a nation. In the Bible, a generation is approximately 40 years. If this is true, then Jesus should have come around 1988! God, however, refers often to His Holy City: Jerusalem. He apparently does not see Israel as a complete nation until they have control of His Holy City. The Jews won control over Jerusalem in 1967. The year 1967 plus 40 years gives us 2007. Thus, Jesus could come back at any time after this date unless there is some other small nuance of prophecy that we're overlooking.

Remember the 70 week prophecy in Daniel? There is a half-week still unaccounted for. This last week was cut in half when the Messiah died in the middle of it. The last part of the prophecy states that a man will make a covenant with the Jews for one week (seven years), but in the midst of the week he will break his promise. This, then, is the missing half-week. The beginning of the last seven years will be marked by the covenant.

> **And he shall speak *great* words against the most High, and shall wear out the saints of the most High, and think to change times and laws: and they shall be given into his hand until a time and times and the dividing of time. (Dan 7:25)**

> But the court which is without the temple leave out, and measure it not; for it is given unto the Gentiles: and the holy city shall they tread under foot forty *and* two months. (Rev 11:2)

> And there was given unto him a mouth speaking great things and blasphemies; and power was given unto him to continue forty *and* two months. (Rev 13:5)

> And the woman fled into the wilderness, where she hath a place prepared of God, that they should feed her there a thousand two hundred *and* threescore days. (Rev 12:6)

We've already discussed the word "times" in Daniel. Time means a year; times means two years; and the dividing of time means ½ of a year, for a total of 3½ years. The 42 months in Revelation also means 3½ years. Finally, the thousand two hundred and threescore days is 1,260 days or exactly 3½ years in 30-day months as required by the Jewish calendar.

This week of seven years is known, by Christians, as the Tribulation. Once the antichrist makes the seven-year covenant with Israel, the Kingdom Age will begin since his identification will be clear. The Jews, however, will be fooled by this covenant. They will identify this man as their long-awaited Messiah. Once the Antichrist sits in the Temple of God, many believing Jews will flee the city of Jerusalem and hide in the wilderness. This event marks the exact middle of the seven years, or 3½ years after his covenant. It's also the event that triggers what evangelicals refer to as the Great Tribulation and the last 3½ years of the antichrist's most ruthless rulership. The woman alluded to in the last prophecy is probably symbolic of the people that was responsible for the birth of the Messiah: Jesus. These are the Jews spoken of by Zechariah who will, obviously, flee to the wilderness after the antichrist claims himself as God and who will welcome Jesus as their Messiah at the Second Coming.

Notice that the Bible says that the antichrist sits in the Temple of God. There is no Temple in Jerusalem today. Historically there have been two Temples. One was built by Solomon and destroyed by the Babylonians. The second was built by Nehemiah, Ezra, Zerubabbel, etc. after their return from captivity in Babylon. It was improved upon by Herod and destroyed by the Romans. The Temple, according to Jewish ceremonial law, can only be rebuilt on the one spot on the Temple Mount (Mount Moriah) designated for it. There are now several movements in Israel to rebuild their ancient site. Almost all of the ancient Temple vessels have been rebuilt; perfect, unspotted red heifers are being raised to purify the Temple site (red heifer ashes are needed to purify the Temple site according to the Law of Moses); all of the building stones are ready; many of the Tribe of Levi have been discovered and trained in the priestly rites; religious Jews, especially from the organization called the Temple Mount Faithful, have been pressuring the Israeli government to allow them to rebuild. With all these things in place, it has been estimated that, once the go-ahead is given, the Temple could be up and operational within six months!

The Antichrist

Who is this Antichrist, and why will God allow him to exist and exercise his power? The first mention of him in the Bible goes all the way back to the third chapter of the Book of Genesis, back in the Protevangelium.

> **And I will put enmity between thee and the woman, and between thy seed and her seed; it shall bruise thy head, and thou shalt bruise his heel. (Gen 3:15)**

I have repeated this important verse here for the reader's convenience. Once again, God is speaking to the serpent and to Lucifer who has possessed the serpent. With the Fall of man, Satan usurped control over the earth and its creatures since man no longer demonstrated the moral capacity to do so. Without a replacement from God immediately ready, Satan stepped into the breach. God allowed this but only in a limited capacity. God would also allow Satan, in the future, to rule over the entire earth through a substitute called the serpent's seed. He would allow this to demonstrate to His entire Creation (i.e., the angels) that Satan has an even less moral capacity to rule the earth than man. This seed (remember, the Hebrew word translated "seed" in this passage is in the singular) must be a man. Since Satan does not possess God's power of Creativity, he must control this man through voluntary satanic possession. I shall attempt to prove this as we progress.

This conflict between the woman's offspring (i.e., God's anointed seed) and the serpent's seed is mentioned in virtually every book of the Bible. It is very important to understand this in order to understand the message of the Bible.

Skipping way ahead in history, the Holy Land (i.e., Israel), and especially the Holy City (i.e., Jerusalem), eventually came under the auspices of Alexander the Great. After Alexander's death, his empire was split amongst his four greatest generals. We shall see, shortly, that this very thing was prophesied in the Bible hundreds of years before it happened. One of Alexander's generals was named Seleucus and took over the far eastern part of the empire. After much conflict with the Ptolemies, who took over the southern part of the empire including Egypt, Israel finally came under control of the Seleucids. One of the Seleucids, named Antiochus Epiphanes, became so enraged with the Ptolemies, that he decided to attack Egypt. On his way to Egypt, he encountered the rebellious Jews who wished to return the rule of their land to a Jewish ruler. This was a petty annoyance to Antiochus who had bigger game in mind in Egypt. On his way, the Romans, who were now coming into prominence as a military power, sent an emissary to Antiochus in Israel warning him not to attack Egypt since the Romans were in an alliance with Egypt. Afraid to proceed any further, and in utter rage because his plans were now thwarted, he vented his rage on the rebellious Jews. He attacked them, put down their rebellion, and violated the sanctity of the Jewish Holy Temple by slaughtering a pig (an unclean animal to the Jews) on the altar in the Temple's Holy of Holies. Simply by entering the Temple, as a Gentile, he desecrated the Temple. But, as we can see, he went much farther, showing the inability of the Jews to stop him from performing such an irreligious and blasphemous act against the Jews' holiest site. Let's see what Daniel had to say about this important event hundreds of years before it happened.

> **And arms shall stand on his part, and they shall pollute the sanctuary of strength, and shall take away the daily sacrifice, and they shall place the abomination that maketh desolate. (Dan 11:31)**

Now, let's see what Nelson's Illustrated Bible Dictionary has to say about him under the separate headings of Antiochus and Epiphanes.

> ANTIOCHUS
>
> 3. Antiochus IV (175-164 B. C.), surnamed Epiphanes (God manifest) but called by his enemies Epimanes (madman). Antiochus IV was one of the cruelest rulers of all time. Like his father, Antiochus III the Great, he was enterprising and ambitious; however, he had a tendency to cruelty that bordered on madness. His primary aim-- to unify his empire by spreading Greek civilization and culture-- brought him into direct conflict with the Jews. This conflict broke into open rebellion in 167 B. C. Accounts of these conflicts are found in the apocryphal book of 2 Maccabees.

The revolt began with Antiochus' edict that sought to unite all the peoples of his kingdom in religion, law, and custom. The Jews were the only people who would not adhere to this edict. Antiochus issued regulations against observing the Sabbath, practicing circumcision, and keeping all food laws. These regulations were followed by the ABOMINATION OF DESOLATION <Dan. 11:31>-- the erection of the altar of the Greek god Zeus over the altar of the burnt offering in the Temple. Jews were forced to participate in heathen festivities and were put to death if they were caught with the Book of the Law in their possession.

As the revolt, led by Judas Maccabeus, gained momentum, the people of Israel united to overthrow Seleucid domination of their land. The Syrians were routed and the Temple was cleansed on the 25th of Chislev, 165 B. C. This cleansing is now observed by the Jews as the Feast of Lights (Hanukkah), around December 25. According to ancient writers, Antiochus IV withdrew into the East following his defeat. He died in Persia a madman. Some scholars see the "little horn" of <Daniel 8:9> as a reference to Antiochus IV Epiphanes.

> EPIPHANES
>
> [e PIFF uh knees]-- a shorter name for Antiochus IV, the king of Syria (reigned 175-163 B. C.). He defiled the Jewish Temple in Jerusalem by sacrificing swine on the altar and by setting himself up as a god to be worshiped. Also see ANTIOCHUS.

This person, in history, is what scholars call a "type" of the antichrist. These very actions, performed by Antiochus Epiphanes, will be repeated by the antichrist. Because the phrase "the son of perdition" is used to describe both only Judas Iscariot and the antichrist, there are some scholars who believe that Judas will be resurrected as the Antichrist.

> **While I was with them in the world, I kept them in thy name: those that thou gavest me I have kept, and none of them is lost, but the son of perdition; that the scripture might be fulfilled. (John 17:12)**

> **Let no man deceive you by any means: for that day shall not come, except there come a falling away first, and that man of sin be revealed, the son of perdition; (II Th 2:3)**

The first quote, from the Gospel of John, is Jesus' quotation concerning Judas Iscariot. The second quote, from 2 Thessalonians, is from Paul telling the Thessalonian believers that the Day of the Lord (i.e., the Tribulation) will not come until the Antichrist is revealed.

The Greek prefix, anti, means two things: against and a substitute. Thus, there are those who believe that this antichrist will not only oppose Christ but imitate Him for the world. Just as Jesus began His ministry at 30 years of age, many believe the antichrist will also be approximately 30. Just as Jesus is the King of the Jews, the antichrist will claim the same. Just as Jesus is one of the three Persons of the Godhead, the antichrist will be accompanied by the False Prophet (a mysterious religious biblical figure who imitates the role of the Holy Spirit) and Satan (who imitates the role of the Father).

Let's, now, go into some of the other characteristics of the antichrist.

> And he shall speak great words against the most High, and shall wear out the saints of the most High, and think to change times and laws: and they shall be given into his hand until a time and times and the dividing of time. (Dan 7:25)

Here Daniel is saying that the Antichrist will blaspheme openly against God, persecute His saints (i.e., believers), and change "times and laws". Whatever this means is obscure, but some scholars believe it means he'll change the calendar and classical holidays.

Daniel also says:

> And in the latter time of their kingdom, when the transgressors are come to the full, a king of fierce countenance, and understanding dark sentences, shall stand up. And his power shall be mighty, but not by his own power: and he shall destroy wonderfully, and shall prosper, and practise, and shall destroy the mighty and the holy people. And through his policy

> also he shall cause craft to prosper in his hand; and he shall magnify himself in his heart, and by peace shall destroy many: he shall also stand up against the Prince of princes; but he shall be broken without hand. (Dan 8:23-25)

The phrases "understanding dark sentences" and "but not by his own power" literally mean that his satanic powers will be complete. Notice that Daniel says "by peace shall destroy many". In other words, he will sign a covenant with the Jews for seven years. Obviously, the covenant that the antichrist makes with Israel for seven years is a peace treaty. Whatever the contents of this treaty, one thing seems likely: the Jews will be able to reconstruct their Temple on the Temple Mount! Many scholars believe that the failed invasion of Israel, which comes from the north and is prophesied in Ezekiel Chapters 38 to 39, will destroy the now present opposition against the Jews from rebuilding their ancient and Holy edifice. This invasion, therefore, must precede the antichrist's peace treaty. A thoroughly documented book to read on this is The Silence is Broken by Douglas Berner.

Daniel has some more interesting facts about the Antichrist.

> And in his estate shall stand up a vile person, to whom they shall not give the honour of the kingdom: but he shall come in peaceably, and obtain the kingdom by flatteries. (Dan 11:21)

> And the king shall do according to his will; and he shall exalt himself, and magnify himself above every god, and shall speak marvellous things against the God of gods, and shall prosper till the indignation be accomplished: for that that is determined shall be done. Neither shall he regard the God of his fathers, nor the desire of women, nor regard any god: for he shall magnify himself above all. But in his estate shall he honour the God of forces: and a god whom his fathers knew not shall he honour with gold, and silver, and with precious stones, and pleasant things.

> Thus shall he do in the most strong holds with a strange god, whom he shall acknowledge and increase with glory: and he shall cause them to rule over many, and shall divide the land for gain. (Dan 11:36-39)

The first passage tells us how the antichrist will come into power: "by flatteries". He will disarm and overwhelm his opposition by flattering them! The second quote says that he will not regard the "God of his fathers". This interpretation has been much disputed. Strong's Concordance tells us that the Hebrew word "'el" is used here. This can only mean God in the singular. In Daniel's time, the only believers were Jews. There were not, as yet, any Christians. Besides, Daniel would certainly *not* concern himself over the possibility that the antichrist would not regard some other idolatrous god such as Baal. To this writer, this can only mean that the antichrist will be a Jew! How else could he convince the nation of Israel that he was their Messiah who is prophesied to come from the Jewish Tribe of Judah?

> I am come in my Father's name, and ye receive me not: if another shall come in his own name, him ye will receive. (John 5:43)

This quotation is Jesus telling the Pharisees that they'll accept another Jew in the future who comes in his own name as their Messiah – the antichrist!

His god is the "god of forces". This is an interesting title, indeed, because it is one of the many classical titles accorded to Lucifer! Furthermore, the phrase "nor the desire of women" identifies him as a man who cannot be mingled in adulterous relationships with women. This, however, does *not* mean that he will be a homosexual! Finally, notice that he shall "divide the land for gain". It has been reported that Yitzhak Rabin entered into a secret pact with the Vatican that was agreed upon by the Islamic nations. This pact would divide Jerusalem, and the Temple Mount, into sections for each of the world's three great monotheistic religions. This would allow the construction of Christian churches and Muslim temples on the Temple Mount. Even now, peace plans are in the works to divide Israel to allow a Palestinian state within their midst such as George W. Bush's Road Map to Peace. More importantly, it would allow the Jews to rebuild their Holy Temple there!

In the middle of the Tribulation, the antichrist will be "slain" and be "resurrected" after three days. Remember, he is a false substitute for Christ. The one who will "resurrect" the antichrist is called "the second beast", or "false prophet" by evangelicals. Who this false prophet is is not as clear as the antichrist since the Bible does not describe him in much detail. Evangelicals believe he will be a religious leader. Whether the antichrist will truly die and be resurrected is a topic of hot debate amongst prophecy buffs. Many believe that this will be a deception since Satan does not have the power of resurrection. Others believe it will be real since the Scriptures do not clearly describe a satanic deception here. Regardless, this marks the time when the antichrist will sit in the Temple of God and declare that he is God. His possession by Satan will then be complete, and God will allow him his 3½ years of rulership over all the earth, including the saints.

> And I stood upon the sand of the sea, and saw a beast rise up out of the sea, having seven heads and ten horns, and upon his horns ten crowns, and upon his heads the name of blasphemy. And the beast which I saw was like unto a leopard, and his feet were as *the feet* of a bear, and his mouth as the mouth of a lion: and the dragon gave him his power, and his seat, and great authority. And I saw one of his heads as it were wounded to death; and his deadly wound was healed: and all the world wondered after the beast. And they worshipped the dragon which gave power unto the beast: and they worshipped the beast, saying, Who *is* like unto the beast? who is able to make war with him? And there was given unto him a mouth speaking great things and blasphemies; and power was given unto him to continue forty *and* two months. And he opened his mouth in blasphemy against God, to blaspheme his name, and his tabernacle, and them that dwell in heaven. And it was given unto him to

> make war with the saints, and to overcome them: and power was given him over all kindreds, and tongues, and nations. (Rev. 13:1-7).

> And I beheld another beast coming up out of the earth; and he had two horns like a lamb, and he spake as a dragon. And he exerciseth all the power of the first beast before him, and causeth the earth and them which dwell therein to worship the first beast, whose deadly wound was healed. (Rev. 13:11-12)

At this midpoint, he will introduce his "mark".

> And he causeth all, both small and great, rich and poor, free and bond, to receive a mark in their right hand, or in their foreheads: And that no man might buy or sell, save he that had the mark, or the name of the beast, or the number of his name. Here is wisdom. Let him that hath understanding count the number of the beast: for it is the number of a man; and his number *is* Six hundred threescore *and* six. (Rev. 13:16-18)

This "mark" is, obviously, an economic mark because no one will be able to buy or sell without it. What is more important is what God says about those who receive this mark.

> And the third angel followed them, saying with a loud voice, If any man worship the beast and his image, and receive *his* mark in his forehead, or in his hand, The same shall drink of the wine of the wrath of God, which is poured out without mixture into the cup of his indignation; and he shall be tormented with fire and brimstone in the presence of the holy angels, and in the presence of the Lamb: And the smoke of their torment ascendeth up for ever and ever: and they have no rest day nor night, who worship the beast and his image, and whosoever receiveth the mark of his name. (Rev. 14:9-11)

Why would a loving, caring God condemn those to eternal Hell who have been deceived into taking the mark of the beast? Once again, I believe the Lord has revealed this to me even though the Bible is silent about this. Anyone who has studied the New Age Movement in any detail will understand why the mark of the beast is so important to God. The New Age Movement has claimed that their Age of Aquarius must commence with what they call "The Luciferic Invocation". This "invocation" is a statement of belief and worship of Lucifer (Satan). What is an invocation? It is a prayer or a summons to Lucifer to come and take control. I have seen some proposed "invocations", and all of them denounce Jesus and accept Satan as their God. Thus, I believe that the mark will only be given to those who are willing to recite this Luciferic Invocation. If this is true, then it's no wonder that God will disown anyone taking the mark since they will have openly rejected Jesus and accepted Lucifer as their God!

As already mentioned, the first 3½ years of the Day of the Lord are known as the Tribulation. This is the time that the antichrist will consolidate his power. The rider on the white horse of the Apocalypse is described as having a bow in his hand but no arrows (Rev. 6:2). The fact that the Scriptures say that the rider is conquering without arrows suggests to many that the rider is definitely the antichrist who is conquering through peace treaties and not forcibly. The second half of the 7 day week of years is known as the Great Tribulation and will be hell on earth. This is the time of Revelation's trumpet, bowl, and vial judgments on mankind. In fact, it will be so bad that it caused Jesus to remark:

> **For then shall be great tribulation, such as was not since the beginning of the world to this time, no, nor ever shall be. And except those days should be shortened, there should no flesh be saved: but for the elect's sake those days shall be shortened. (Matt. 24:21-22)**

As already alluded to, Jesus will return to the earth at His Second Advent, protect the now-believing Jews, defeat the antichrist and his armies, throw Lucifer and the fallen angels into the great pit and the Nephilim, the antichrist, the false prophet, and all unbelieving humans into a lake of molten fire to be punished for their extreme wickedness for eternity, and end the Great Tribulation.

The Millennium

The Millennium (or, literally, one thousand years) is a time when Jesus Christ shall rule the entire Earth. He will not do this forcefully; only Israel shall be taken over by force. Instead, each nation that survives the Tribulation will voluntarily join Jesus' Kingdom. This can be seen by Jesus' parable of the mustard seed growing into a giant tree in the Gospels.

> Another parable put he forth unto them, saying, The kingdom of heaven is like to a grain of mustard seed, which a man took, and sowed in his field: Which indeed is the least of all seeds: but when it is grown, it is the greatest among herbs, and becometh a tree, so that the birds of the air come and lodge in the branches thereof. (Matt 13:31-32)

Notice that Jesus purposely likens His "kingdom of heaven" to a "mustard seed". A mustard seed is one of the smaller seeds that grows into a full-blown tree. In other words, the kingdom will begin small (with only the state of Israel) and grow greatly. Once the Tribulation has ended, the only people left on Earth will be believers. They, believing in Him, will *want* to join His kingdom. The blessings that Jesus will pour on the Jewish nation will also make all the other nations wish to partake in these blessings. Satan and his demons will be chained for the thousand years.

> And I saw an angel come down from heaven, having the key of the bottomless pit and a great chain in his hand. And he laid hold on the dragon, that old serpent, which is the Devil, and Satan, and bound him a thousand years, (Rev 20:1-2)

God, at this time will establish His New Covenant which is, obviously, unconditional.

> Behold, the days come, saith the LORD, that I will make a new covenant with the house of Israel, and with the house of Judah: Not according to the covenant that I made with their fathers in the day that I took them by the hand to bring them out of the land of Egypt; which my covenant they brake, although I was an husband unto them, saith the LORD: But this shall be the covenant that I will make with the house of Israel; After those days, saith the LORD, I will put my law in their inward parts, and write it in their hearts; and will be their God, and they shall be my people. And they shall teach no more every man his neighbour, and every man his brother, saying, Know the LORD: for they shall all know me, from the least of them unto the greatest of them, saith the LORD: for I will forgive their iniquity, and I will remember their sin no more. (Jer 31:31-34)

The Jews will, once again, become God's people. They will no longer sin against the Lord.

The longevity of people's lives to a thousand years in duration, which was prevalent before the Flood, will be restored.

> For, behold, I create new heavens and a new earth: and the former shall not be remembered, nor come into mind. But be ye glad and rejoice for ever in that which I create: for, behold, I create Jerusalem a rejoicing, and her people a joy. And I will rejoice in Jerusalem, and joy in my people: and the voice of weeping shall be no more heard in her, nor the voice of crying. There shall be no more thence an infant of days, nor an old man that hath not filled his days: for the child shall die an hundred years old; but the sinner being an hundred years old shall be accursed. And they shall

> build houses, and inhabit them; and they shall plant vineyards, and eat the fruit of them. They shall not build, and another inhabit; they shall not plant, and another eat: for as the days of a tree are the days of my people, and mine elect shall long enjoy the work of their hands. They shall not labour in vain, nor bring forth for trouble; for they are the seed of the blessed of the LORD, and their offspring with them. And it shall come to pass, that before they call, I will answer; and while they are yet speaking, I will hear. The wolf and the lamb shall feed together, and the lion shall eat straw like the bullock: and dust shall be the serpent's meat. They shall not hurt nor destroy in all my holy mountain, saith the LORD. (Isa 65:17-25)

Notice that childhood shall last a hundred years. There will be no more weeping and sorrow. Everyone will enjoy the fruits of his own labor without the worry of confiscation from banks, the government, or others. Animals will once again become vegetarians. Peace will reign throughout the world. The saints (i.e., the true Church) will rule with Jesus. The Jews will become the most prestigious ethnic group in the world. Once more, the tree of life will become available to the saints.

As great as all this sounds, it is still not the end of God's Plan. Remember, this is merely the seventh dispensation; it must also end.

End of the Millennium

At the end of the Millennium, Satan will be released to deceive the people once again at the end of the thousand years..

> And cast him into the bottomless pit, and shut him up, and set a seal upon him, that he should deceive the nations no more, till the thousand years should be fulfilled: and after that he must be loosed a little season. (Rev 20:3)

Since the Millennium will have begun with nothing but believers, Satan's deceptions would seem to be fruitless. But during the thousand years, the believers will have offspring. Not all of these offspring will be saved, but many will pretend to be since Salvation will be the norm of the day. Satan's deceptions will uncover these unsaved people showing the world who they are. Satan will organize them to attempt to overthrow Jesus' Throne. This is necessary in God's overall Plan to convince His loyal angels that no ordinary man, even with all the attendant blessings bestowed on him, is morally capable of ruling the Earth.

> And when the thousand years are expired, Satan shall be loosed out of his prison, And shall go out to deceive the nations which are in the four quarters of the earth, Gog and Magog, to gather them together to battle: the number of whom is as the sand of the sea. And they went up on the breadth of the earth, and compassed the camp of the saints about, and the beloved city: and fire came down from God out of heaven, and devoured them. (Rev 20:7-9)

Once God's fire consumes them, Satan will be thrown into the lake of fire forever; all unbelievers will be resurrected to face their final Judgment at the Great White Throne; Jesus will give His Throne over to the Father; the Plan of God will finally be realized; and the "Age of ages", or eternity, will begin.

> And the devil that deceived them was cast into the lake of fire and brimstone, where the beast and the false prophet are, and shall be tormented day and night for ever and ever. And I saw a great white throne, and him that sat on it, from whose face the earth and the heaven fled away; and there was found no place for them. And I saw the dead, small and great, stand before God; and the books were opened: and another book was opened, which is the book of life: and the dead were judged out of those things which were written in the books, according to their works.

> And the sea gave up the dead which were in it; and death and hell delivered up the dead which were in them: and they were judged every man according to their works. And death and hell were cast into the lake of fire. This is the second death.
>
> And whosoever was not found written in the book of life was cast into the lake of fire. (Rev 20:10-15)

Between the Millennium and eternity, judgment must be meted out to the unjust. This judgment, known as the Great White Throne Judgment, will be based on works and not Jesus' substitutionary death. The Judgment of the righteous occurred years before at the Rapture. Since none of these judged at this time, including the fallen angels and Nephilim, ever had faith in Jesus' sacrifice, none of them will be saved.

Chapter 11

CONCLUSION

I've often wondered whether most "Christians" take the Gospel as some kind of magical incantation. How many of these "Christians" have ever demonstrated a truly changed lifestyle? And what of other religions? For example, would a Muslim come to Allah in tears and repentance? How about Shiva, Buddha, or even Lucifer?

Before I was saved, I was not totally convinced that someone called Jesus ever truly walked the earth or was merely some all-encompassing "idea" to separate men from their money. When I was first exposed to the workplace, there were some co-workers who were constantly trying to proselytize me to Christianity. Even though I was impressed with their insistence, they were never able to answer even the simplest questions revolving around in my mind. I was definitely not one to begin bawling emotionally like a child over someone's perceived "truth". To my credit, I respected their beliefs enough and realized their perceived concern for me so that I never complained about their proselytizing to higher management even though I respectfully asked them to stop.

Once I became aware that I couldn't even trust my teachers to give me the truth without bias, I began to seek it elsewhere. My search astounded me. I was wrong about everything I believed! Eventually, it led me to Jesus.

> Ask, and it shall be given you; seek, and ye shall find; knock, and it shall be opened unto you: For every one that asketh receiveth; and he that seeketh findeth; and to him that knocketh it shall be opened. (Matt 7:7-8)

What a wonderful promise! God (i.e., Jesus) will allow anyone to discover the truth who seeks it honestly. I began to find that many things that I once solidly believed in were not really so solid. In fact, most of them were dead wrong. I discovered that the Pentateuch had a good, scientific basis for the miracles recorded. I also discovered that the Ten Commandments were actually a solid basis for mankind to live in freedom. One by one, the claims of the Scriptures became validated in my mind. As these things became true to me incrementally, what of the many claims in the Bible that couldn't be verified such as Creation? Even though I could not substantiate the account of the Creation, what could I do with its antithesis: evolution? The more I delved into evolutionary claims, the more I realized that it, too, was merely a religion that denied God. There were actually *no* facts to validate its authenticity.

What then of other biblical claims such as the virgin conception of Jesus, the deity of Jesus, etc.? As wild as these claims are, there are actual historical accounts that verify them. Many contemporary authors with Jesus report them.

I was brought to a quandary. Do I reject all of this evidence and continue to live in my own comfortable way? Or do I accept them and realize that the truth requires a life-changing experience? At first, I continued to ask embarrassing, but valid, questions. Perhaps I was hoping that the truth may not have been the truth at all. But just as God promised, He led me to the answers to my questions and didn't allow me to shrink back into my unbelieving, comfortable world. He did this in many ways: prayer, reading the Bible, and reading authors who had written books with which I could find no fault and, eventually, came to trust them.

Because I have asked the hard questions and received the hard answers, He also placed the idea of biblical apology in my heart. I believe He did this so that I would feel compelled to share many of these things with you. Even though I have tried to introduce some of the concepts that I've learned, those recorded herein are nowhere near exhaustive. For further questions, the true Christian should try to seek out answers anywhere he can find them such as many of the other works I've cited.

Hopefully, I have demonstrated that the truths that can be shown to be true probably are with a great probability of certainty. If this is so, the biblical claims that can not be proven should be seriously considered by anyone who is truly honest. Also, I pray that this manuscript honors, reverences, and glorifies the Lord who has bought me at such a high price.

There is a point of knowledge and truth at which unbelief requires more faith than Christianity. I believe that much of the evidence presented in this book has, at least, approached that point. If the reader is truly honest and sincere in his quest for the truth then he will, at least, consult some of the other works mentioned herein. The sum total of the truths presented in these other manuscripts will definitely pass that point just mentioned.

Selected Bibliography

The following bibliography is meant to give the reader the knowledge to look up the texts from which I've gleaned much of the information I've used in writing this book. It is by no means exhaustive. There are hundreds of other writings that could have just as easily been included here. I encourage the reader to search through the books included here plus the many other books that supplement these. Furthermore, I have purposely included some of my own notes on these books so that the reader can decide on his own whether a book included here will titillate the reader's curiosity.

------, Biblical Archaeological Review (A periodical magazine that continuously updates biblical archaeology.)

------, Nelson's Bible Dictionary, Thomas Nelson Publishers, copyright 1986

------, New Schofield Reference Bible, Oxford University Press, copyright 1967

------, The Lost Books of the Bible, Meridian, copyright 1926, first printing November, 1974 (This book contains the Epistle of Barnabbas.)

------, Josephus, Antiquities of the Jews, Kregel Publications, copyright 1981 (A Jewish historian who lived in the time of Jesus and recounts the Old Testament accounts that were believed in that day.)

Anderson, Sir Robert, The Coming Prince, Kregel Publications, copyright 1984 (A classic in Christian literature! Anderson, a retired Scotland Yard Inspector, researched the dating of the Artaxerxes decree and painstakingly calculated the end date of the 69 weeks of years as prophesied in Daniel.)

Bates, Gary, Alien Intrusion, Master Books, copyright 2004, third printing May, 2005 (A well-written and researched book into the veracity of the current UFO hype. Bates strips away the emotion around the history of UFOs including Roswell, alien autopsies, and Area 51 and forms purely logical conclusions. His last conclusion is remarkable.)

Berner, Douglas, The Silence is Broken, (no publisher given), copyright 2006 (This book researches the biblical prophecy of the so-called "War of Gog and Magog" found in Ezekiel 38 & 39, makes educated guesses as to the major players in the prophecy, compares these chapters to other biblical references, and comes to some astounding conclusions.)

Brooke, Tal, Lord of the Air, Harvest House Publications, copyright 1991 (This is the story, alluded to in the text, about the author's acquaintance with Indian guru Sai Baba. An interesting account that's well written.)

Church, J. R., Prophecy in the News dated February, 1999 Home of the Soul (Dr. Church makes some interesting observations about the definition and meaning of the human soul.)

Church, J.R., Prophecy in the News dated June, 2010 Has Noah's Ark Been Found at Last? (Drs. J. R. Church and Gary Stearman interview Arch Bonnema about his discovery of Noah's Ark on Mt. Suleiman in northern Iran. The article reveals finds and pictures from the site.)

Cornuke, Robert and Halbrook, David, The Lost Mountain of Noah, Broadman and Holman Publishers, copyright 2001 (These two adventurers have questioned the classical location of Mt. Ararat as the resting place for Noah's Ark and explored a mountain in northwestern Iran as a promising site.)

Cornuke, Robert and Williams, Larry, The Search for the Real Mt. Sinai, video from the Explorer Series, ordered at www.monumentpictures.com, or call 1-800-680-3300 (An incredible discovery! Not only have these men discovered the real Mt. Sinai, but they've discovered other sites that are recorded in the Book of Exodus. This not only reveals the true path of the Jewish journey to the mountain, but it also reveals their probable exit from the Sinai Peninsula across the Red Sea.)

Cumbey, Constance, The Hidden Dangers of the Rainbow Huntington House, copyright 1983, Revised Edition (A Christian classic on the New Age Movement.)

Dillow, Joseph C., Reign of the Servant Kings, Schoettle Publishing Co., copyright 1992, second edition 1993 (A well detailed and scholarly work that resolves the difference in arguments between Arminianism and Calvinism. According to Dr. Dillow both sides are wrong but very close in their explanation of salvation and eternal security. The answer is sanctification, and Dr. Dillow does an excellent job of clearing up the differences, explaining otherwise difficult Scriptural passages, and shows how the Christian can be fully sanctified in this life. This work, although more than 600 pages, is a must for the serious Christian.)

Dillow, Joseph C., The Waters Above, Moody Press, copyright 1981, 1982 (A highly technical book that attempts to support, scientifically, his hypothesis of a 40 foot thick water vapor canopy that enveloped the earth before the Flood.)

Drosnin, Michael, The Bible Code, Simon and Schuster, copyright 1997 (A journalist looks at the Bible codes to publicize them. Even though most reputable mathematicians have discounted much of Drosnin's conclusions, he is the one responsible for bringing the Bible codes to the public's attention.)

Gibbon, Edward, The Decline and Fall of the Roman Empire, Abridged Version, Bonanza Books, copyright MCMLX, 1985 edition (The version I have of this book is abridged. Chapters 15 and 16, however, were copied wholly intact. This is because these two chapters are the most important in the entire work because they treat the rise of Christianity in the Roman Empire.)

Gitt, Werner, In the Beginning Was Information, Master Books, copyright 2005, first printing February, 2006 (A highly technical book written in the sense of Euclid's axiomatic method. The conclusions, however, point to the existence of God.)

Good, Joseph, Rosh Hashanah and the Messianic Kingdom to Come, Hatikva Ministries, copyright 1989 (A great composition that backs the argument, from a Jewish perspective, that the Rapture must occur on a Rosh Hashanah.)

Hislop, Alexander, The Two Babylons, Loizeaux Brothers, second edition 1959 (This book is not only a Christian classic but a *must-read* for every true Christian! It is hard to read because Hislop traces all the names of all the gods through every culture, religion, and generation from the Tower of Babel until today. He shows that all of the beliefs of the ancient Babylonian religion are held, and practiced, in today's Roman Catholic Church.)

Jeffrey, Grant R., Creation, Frontier Research Publications, copyright 2003 (An interesting read that confirms God's creative handiwork in all spheres of learning.)

Jeffrey, Grant R., The Signature of God, Frontier Research Publications, copyright 1996 (In this book, Grant shows how many writings are still extant today that proves the veracity of the Bible that the public knows nothing about.)

Missler, Chuck and Eastman, Mark, Alien Encounters, Koinonia House, copyright 1999, fifth printing January, 2003 (A scientific and theological look at the possibility that the Genesis 6 passage speaks of giants.)

Missler, Chuck, Cosmic Codes, Koinonia House, copyright 1999, Revised 2004 (If the reader can get past the first two chapters, this book is an excellent read that treats many hidden concepts contained in the Bible.)

Missler, Chuch and Nancy, The Kingdom, Power, & Glory, The King's Highway Ministries, In., copyright 2007, second printing (This book is centered on the personal responsibility of sanctification for *every* Christian. It is full of charts and explanations that even the least informed Christian should be able to understand. Because the doctrine of sanctification is so vital to the Christian's life, this book is another must read. It can be ordered online at http://store.khouse.org or by telephone at 1-800-KHOUSE-1 [546-8731].)

Missler, Chuck, Personal Update for September 2006, Volume 16, No. 9 Written for a Generation to Come (An article designed to show how geneticists actually prove the biblical truth of Adam and Eve.)

Missler, Chuck, Personal Update, Volume 9, No. 1, January 1999 Speed of Light Slowing Down? (An article questioning the constancy of the speed of light and, thereby, bringing into question Einstein's Theory of Relativity.)

Montgomery, John Warwick, The Quest for Noah's Ark, Pyramid Books, copyright 1972, second printing March, 1975 (An historical account of attempts to verify that Noah's Ark rests upon Mount Ararat in Turkey.)

Moore, George Foot, Judaism, Hendrickson Publishers, copyright 1927, first printing March, 1997 (A two volume tome of the laws, rituals, customs, culture, etc. that affected the devout Jew in the first century.)

Moore, Philip, The End of History: Messiah Conspiracy, Ramshead Press International, Copyright 1996 (A monumental work! Dr. Moore goes back to ancient Jewish commentaries to document their interpretations of early messianic prophecies in the Old Testament and compares them to modern Jewish interpretations to demonstrate the unbelievable bias against the acceptance of Jesus as the Jewish Messiah. I highly recommend this book.)

Morison, Frank, Who Moved the Stone?, Lamplighter Books (Zondervan), first printing 1958 (A Christian classic documenting the author's reasoning for his conversion to Christianity.)

Morris, Henry M., A Symposium on Creation, Baker Book House, copyright 1968, fifth printing February, 1976 (A compilation of different Christian authors on several topics involving Creation.)

Morris, Henry M., The Biblical Basis for Modern Science, Baker Book House, copyright 1984 (Doctor Henry M. Morris of the Institute for Creation Research shows how the biblical record is vindicated by modern science and vice-versa.)

Morris, Henry M., The Genesis Record, Baker Book House, copyright 1976, eleventh printing August, 1986 (A scientist and believer interprets the Book of Genesis.)

Patten, Donald W., A Symposium on Creation II, Baker Book House, copyright 1970, third printing November, 1974, Donald W. Patten The Pre-Flood Greenhouse Effect (How the world before the Flood affected life.)

Patten, Donald W., A Symposium on Creation III, Baker Book House, copyright 1971, third printing April, 1977

Patten, Donald W., A Symposium on Creation IV, Baker Book House, copyright 1972, second printing February, 1976

Patten, Donald W., A Symposium on Creation V, Baker Book House, copyright 1975

Price, Randall, The Stones Cry Out, Harvest House Publishers, copyright 1997 (Archaeological discoveries that confirm the biblical record.)

Quayle, Stephen, Aliens & Fallen Angels, End Time Thunder Publishers, copyright 2008 (An excellent work that reveals Satan's past and present deceptions and his current work to deceive mankind in the not-too-distant future. I had a hard time putting this work down.)

Quayle, Stephen, Genesis 6 Giants, End Time Thunder Publishers, copyright 2005 (Even though I disagree with the author's conclusion of a pre-adamic race, the research behind this book is exhaustive, and his other conclusions, which are compelling, are astounding. For example, he recounts historical events which, if they're true, demonstrate a purposeful cover-up of history.)

Rambsel, Yacov, Yeshua, Frontier Research Publications, copyright 1996 (A Jewish convert to Christianity uses Equidistant Letter Sequences manually to find Jesus' name hidden in the Old Testament.)

Satinover, Jeffrey, Cracking the Bible Code, William Morrow & Company, copyright 1997 (An account of how one of the world's leading cryptanalysts and mathematicians confirmed the authenticity of the Bible codes based on probability and statistics. This book is not an easy read.)

Seiss, Joseph, The Witness of the Stars (An account of how the original signs of the zodiac portray the prophetic Plan of God.)

Sherman, R. Edwin, Bible Code Bombshell New Leaf Press, copyright 2005, second printing May, 2006 (A renowned mathematician, together with a small team of other experts, recently discovered hundreds of Bible Codes in a small number of biblical passages. The author then documents his findings with the probabilities of finding these codes.)

Strong, James, Strong's Hebrew/Greek Concordance, Thomas Nelson Publishers, published 1980

Varner, William, Jacob's Dozen, Friends of Israel Gospel Ministry, copyright 1987, first printing 1993 (A look at the prophecies and blessings that Jacob bestows on his 12 children at the end of the Book of Genesis.)

Velikovsky, Immanuel, Earth in Upheaval, Pocket Books, copyright 1955 (A look at the extraterrestrial possibilities for the biblical account of the Flood.)

Velikovsky, Immanuel, Worlds in Collision, Pocket Books, copyright 1950, first printing March, 1977 (A classic! Velikovsky documents his discoveries that both the Old and New Testament miracles had their origins in extraterrestrial events. This book is not an easy read because Dr. Velikovsky attempts to verify his conclusions to the scientific community.)

Whitcomb John C., & Morris, Henry M., The Genesis Flood, Presbyterian Reformed Publishing Company, copyright 1961 (A classic! Whitcomb, a theologian, and Morris, a scientist, demonstrate the fallacy of the uniformitarian basis for the present condition of the earth. All of the present geological formations of the earth, they claim, can be accounted for by onrushing waters such as those which occurred during the Flood. This is not an easy read because the authors attempt to present these ideas to the scientific community and, as such, they cover all the aspects of their thesis.)

Willmington, Harold L., The Doctrine of Man, (no publisher given), copyright 1977 (A theologian discusses one of the main Christian doctrines.)

Other Helpful Texts

This part of the bibliography is to assist the reader, who wishes to know more, to find other helpful references that have helped me.

Baer, Randall N., Inside the New Age Movement, Huntington House Publications, copyright 1989

deParrie, Paul and Pride, Mary, Ancient Empires of the New Age, Crossway Books, copyright 1989, third printing 1990

Heron, Patrick, The Nephilim and the Pyramid of the Apocalypse, Xulon Press, copyright 2005 (Mr. Heron believes that the nephilim built the pyramids and other ancient monuments that cannot be duplicated by the men of today. He further claims that ancient depictions of eagles with lion's heads, men with the head of jackals, etc. were not imaginary creatures but the product of DNA manipulation conducted by nephilim and fallen angels.)

Horn, Thomas R., Nephilim Stargates, Anomalos Publishing, copyright 2007 (The author claims that fallen angels use "stargates", much like the current fad about the existence of wormholes, to come to the current dimension that the Earth is in. He supports the ancient stories that the first fallen angels of Genesis 6 entered the Earth at Mount Hermon in today's country of Lebanon.)

Hunt, Dave, In Defense of the Faith, Harvest House Publishers, copyright 1996 (Dave Hunt is truly one of the most gifted Christian writers today. His logic is always straightforward, above reproach, and his conclusions are compelling. This listing was given because it's a good work in apologetics.)

Jeffrey, Grant R., The Handwriting of God, Frontier Research Publications, copyright 1997

Lawrence, Troy, New Age Messiah Identified?, Huntington House Publications, copyright 1991 (An educated attempt at identifying the so-called "Maitreya" of the New Age.)

Lindsey, Hal and Carlson, C. C., The Late. Great Planet Earth, Zondervan, copyright 1970 (This work is a Christian classic. Lindsey covers prophecy in a way that's both humorous and layman-oriented. His title caught the eye of many of the curious and was single-handedly responsible for the conversion of many people.)

Lindsey, Hal, Vanished Into Thin Air, Western Front, copyright 1999 (An interesting discourse on the Christian doctrine of the Rapture.)

MacBeth, Norman, Darwin Retried, Gambit Incorporated, copyright 1971 (A former trial judge and committed atheist, MacBeth claims that the onus of proof is on the evolutionists. Whether evolution is true or not doesn't matter – the falseness of evolution says nothing about the truth of Special Creation. He then proceeds to demonstrate that the theory of evolution defies simple logic, breaks all of the rules of the scientific method, and cannot be demonstrated as true based on the fossil record.)

Marrs, Texe, Dark Secrets of the New Age, Crossway Books, copyright 1987, ninth printing 1988 (All of Texe Marrs books have been invaluable to me. The two listed here are merely references as a start to purchase all of his books.)

Marrs, Texe, Ravaged by the New Age, Living Truth Publishers, copyright 1989

Pentecost, J. Dwight, Things to Come, Academic Books (Zondervan), copyright 1958 (This book is a Christian classic! Detailed, but still easily understood by the layman, Doctor Pentecost lays out the major themes of prophecy and answers many of the questions that someone might raise.)

Peters, George N. H., The Theocratic Kingdom, Kregel Publications, copyright 1972 (Originally published in 1884, Doctor Peters' work is a long drawn out and difficult to read compendium of premillennial doctrine. The work is three volumes long and encompasses hundreds of pages. For anyone who really wishes to understand the full tenor of Christianity, premillennialism, and the literal approach to reading the Scriptures, this is a must read!)

Rhodes, Ron, The Counterfeit Christ of the New Age Movement, Baker Book House, copyright 1990, second printing July, 1991

Strobel, Lee, The Case for Christ, Zondervan Publishing House, copyright 1998 (This text confirms the biblical account that Jesus was who He said He was.)

Thompson, J. A., The Bible and Archaeology, William B. Eerdmans Publishing Company, copyright 1962, 1972, 1982, reprinted November, 1988 (A record of archaeological finds that demonstrate the veracity of the Bible.)

Weldon, John, Decoding the Bible Code, Harvest House Publishing, copyright 1998 (Another interesting dialogue on the Bible codes.)